STUDIES IN ROMANCE LANGUAGES: 40

John E. Keller, Editor

REVIEW COPY

May 23, 1996

PUBLICATION DATE
Cloth, $21.95   ISBN: 0-8131-1952-9   200 pages, 5½ x 8½

PRICE

THE PRESENCE OF CAMÕES
Influences on the Literature of
England, America, and Southern Africa
GEORGE MONTEIRO

We would appreciate two copies of your review.

THE UNIVERSITY PRESS OF
KENTUCKY

LEXINGTON, KENTUCKY 40508-4008

The Presence of Camões

Influences on the Literature of England, America, and Southern Africa

GEORGE MONTEIRO

THE UNIVERSITY PRESS OF KENTUCKY

Publication of this book has been assisted by the
Calouste Gulbenkian Foundation.

The following poems are reprinted by permission of the publishers: "One Art"
and "Sonnet" from *The Complete Poems, 1927-1979*, by Elizabeth Bishop, copy-
right © 1979, 1983 by Alice Helen Methfessel, reprinted by permission of Farrar,
Straus & Giroux, Inc. "Gentle spirit mine" from *Louis de Camoëns and the
Epic of the Lusiads*, by Henry H. Hart, copyright © 1962 by the University of
Oklahoma Press. "To His Beloved in Heaven" by Keith Bosley from *Luis de
Camões: Epic & Lyric*, edited by L.C. Taylor, copyright © 1990 by Carcanet
Press.

Copyright © 1996 by The University Press of Kentucky

Scholarly publisher for the Commonwealth,
serving Bellarmine College, Berea College, Centre
College of Kentucky, Eastern Kentucky University,
The Filson Club, Georgetown College, Kentucky
Historical Society, Kentucky State University,
Morehead State University, Murray State University,
Northern Kentucky University, Transylvania University,
University of Kentucky, University of Louisville,
and Western Kentucky University.

Editorial and Sales Offices: The University Press of Kentucky
663 South Limestone Street, Lexington, Kentucky 40508-4008

Library of Congress Cataloging-in-Publication Data
Monteiro, George.
   The Presence of Camões : influences on the literature of England,
America, and Southern Africa / George Monteiro.
      p.   cm.   — (Studies in Romance languages : 40)
   Includes bibliographical references (p.) and index.
   ISBN 0-8131-1952-9 (cloth : alk. paper)
   1. American literature—Portuguese influences. 2. American
literature—History and criticism. 3. Camões, Luís de, 1524?-1580—
Influence. 4. Southern African literature—Portuguese influences.
5. Southern African literature—History and criticism. 6. English
literature—Portuguese influences. 7. English literature—History and
criticism. 8. Portugal—In literature. I. Title. II. Series:
Studies in Romance languges (Lexington, Ky.) : 40.
PS159.P8M66   1996
810.9—dc20   95-46725

This book is printed on acid-free recycled paper meeting
the requirements of the American National Standard
for Permanence of Paper for Printed Library Materials.

Manufactured in the United States of America

Valeu a pena? Tudo vale a pena
Se a alma não é pequena.

— Fernando Pessoa

To the memory of those many emigrants who
became immigrants, including my own,

Augusta Temudo Monteiro
Francisco José Monteiro
Maria Rosa Monteiro Santos
Alfredo Santos
Lucinda Temudo Pestana
Antonio Pestana
Maximina L. Temudo
Antonio Augusto Temudo
Infancia Massa Valente
Joaquim Gomes Valente

Contents

Illustrations

This book is published
with the support of the
Instituto Camões,
Portugal.

Acknowledgments

I wish to thank the editors of journals in which parts of this book have appeared, largely in different form. Those journals are *Revista Camoniana*, *New England Quarterly*, *University of Mississippi Studies in English*, *Studies in Browning and His Circle*, and *Journal of Modern Literature*.

William Blake's painting of Camões is reproduced here from *Heads of the Poets*, a rare 1925 publication of the Blake Society in a run of twenty-five copies. It appears here with the consent of the Beinecke Library, Yale University, which provided me with a reproducible copy. The Houghton Library, Harvard University, Cambridge, Massachusetts, provided me with photographs of the two manuscripts for Melville's diptych poem on Camões and kindly consented to their use here. To the best of my knowledge they have not hitherto been published.

The illustration from Sir Richard Fanshawe's translation of *Os Lusíadas* reproduces the portrait of Camões probably used by Blake as the basis for his own painting. One page from Melville's copy of Lord Strangford's *Poems, from the Portuguese of Luis de Camoens* is reproduced through the kind consent of J.C. Levenson.

Permission to quote the poetry of Roy Campbell was granted by Francisco Campbell Custódio and Ad. Donker (Pty) Ltd. The poetry of Elizabeth Bishop, as well as unpublished material at Vassar College, is quoted by permission of Alice Helen Methfessel and Farrar, Straus and Giroux. Translations of Camões's sonnet "Alma minha gentil" by Jonathan Griffin, Keith Bosley, Henry H. Hart, and Leonard S. Downes are reprinted by permission of, respectively, Menard Press, Carcanet Press, the University of Oklahoma Press, and the Estate of Leonard S. Downes. Efforts to reach A.R. Barter were unsuccessful.

My work on this book has taken me to many libraries over

the years, including the Houghton and Widener Libraries at Harvard University; the Bienecke Library at Yale University; the New York Public Library; the Harry Ransom Humanities Research Center at the University of Texas, Austin; the Homer Babbidge Library, University of Connecticut, Storrs; Special Collections of the Vassar College Libraries; and the Biblioteca Nacional in Lisbon. The staffs at these libraries have been very helpful, but I owe special thanks to my friends at the John Hay Library and the John D. Rockefeller Library at Brown University for helping out with my requests and problems over the short and long haul.

I am also grateful for the encouragement and support of my colleagues and co-workers on all three floors of Meiklejohn House, the home of the Department of Portuguese and Brazilian Studies at Brown University. Of enormous help, too, have been the decades of good friendship and continued talk with David H. Hirsch.

Katherine Monteiro read an earlier version of this study. I am grateful to her, first for giving it her informed scholarly attention, and then for her sagacious suggestions on ways to improve it. I am grateful, too, to Brian Head, whose suggestions for changes and corrections were right to the point, and to José Blanco, who continues to take an informed interest in my work. Brenda Murphy has helped again, more often and in more ways than she can surmise. Thanks.

Introduction

Of the great epic poets in the grand Western tradition, Luis Vaz de Camões remains the least known outside of his native land, and of the premier Western epics, his *Os Lusíadas* enjoys the unenviable distinction of being, hands down, epic poetry's best kept secret. Yet a century and a half after his death Voltaire named Camões the "Portuguese Virgil," and in the nineteenth century he was sometimes called the "Portuguese Plutarch."[1]

Camões has always had the respect of poets and scholars. During the Portuguese poet's lifetime the Italian poet Torquato Tasso dedicated a tributary sonnet to him, and in 1648 the Spanish writer Baltasar Gracián writes of Camões admiringly in his *Agudeza y arte de ingenio*. His poetic eminence was noted by the Spanish dramatist Lope de Vega and poets such as Góngora and Goethe. Writing in the twentieth century, Erich Auerbach calls *Os Lusíadas*, the celebration of Portuguese history and the achievements of the Portuguese people, "the most beautiful epic of the Iberian Peninsula." It is "the great epic of the ocean," he adds, "which sings of Vasco da Gama's voyage around Africa and the Portuguese colonization of the Indies."[2] And C.M. Bowra singles it out as one of four chief examples of the literary epic, the other three being those of Virgil, Tasso, and Milton. In fact, writes Bowra, Camões's work is "the first epic poem which in its grandeur and its universality speaks for the modern world."[3]

The author of *Os Lusíadas* was born around 1524 and died in 1580. The details of much of his life are at best shadowy, but it is widely accepted that his family came from Galicia, that he studied at Coimbra University, and fought as a soldier, losing an eye in Morocco. He was in India, subsequently moving out, over the course of nearly seventeen years in the East, as far as the China seas. When he returned to Portugal in 1570 he brought with him his manuscript of *Os Lusíadas*, dedicated to

1

the young King Sebastian. For his literary efforts—his epic hon-
oring the Portuguese people—and for his other services to the
nation, he was awarded a small pension, too small to sustain
him, though even then it was not paid regularly. Legend has it
that he lived out his few remaining years in poverty and was
given a pauper's burial. Not until 1595 was his substantial corpus of lyric poetry gathered and published under his name.

In his day and for some time afterward Camões's literary
reputation rested on his epic poem. From 1655, when *Os
Lusíadas* appeared in Sir Richard Fanshawe's spirited translation, and running through the eighteenth century, when William J. Mickle re-translated Camões's poem, it was Camões the
epic poet who stood firm in English eyes. William Hayley
warmly praised Mickle's effort, recommending it to the American poet Joel Barlow as a model. John Milton knew *Os Lusíadas*,
probably not in the original but in Fanshawe's translation. Indeed, Milton, as it turned out, was only one of the many English poets whose own work was influenced by Camões's poetry,
epic and lyric. In some sense this is perhaps as it should be.
The adventurer, traveler, student of languages, and compiler of
the so-called "Arabian Nights" (*The Thousand Nights and a
Night*), Sir Richard Burton, thought so, for in 1880 he quoted
with approval the lines of the Portuguese poet Manuel Corrêa:
"Let poets be read by other poets; / Only by other poets be their
/ Divine works elucidated" ("Poetas por poetas sejam lidos; /
Sejam só por poetas explicadas / Suas obras divinas").[4] Corrêa's
lines were useful to Burton in his apology for his own efforts at
"Englishing" the poetry of his "master, Camoens," as he called
him.[5]

In 1880 Burton's version was but the latest in a line of English translations of Camões's epic, preceded by those of the
aforementioned Fanshawe and Mickle, as well as, in the nineteenth century, those of such long-forgotten workers in the vine-
yard as Thomas Moore Musgrave (1826), Edward Quillinan
(1853), T. Livingston Mitchell (1854), J.J. Aubertin (1878), and
Robert Ffrench Duff (1880). The twentieth century has produced
two translations—Leonard Bacon's in verse (1950) and William
C. Atkinson's in prose (1952).

Most of Camões's fame, writes Jorge de Sena, "rested for

long much more on the epic than on the lyric poetry, which, very much admired through the centuries, has only in the last 40 years begun to be understood as the high intellectual achievement that his own times and the 17th century had seen it to be." Sena continues:

> At the end of the 19th century, Camões was thought to be the Renaissance poet and man *par excellence,* after having been, for the European Romantics, a paragon of the adventurous genius who lives unhappy in love and dies a miser [read "in misery"] ignored by society. Today, the notion of the Renaissance proper has shrunk, and it no longer covers with its legendary luminous skies the anguish of Camões, heir to the European High Renaissance, but rather the great Mannerist frustrated by a time 'out of joint' (as he called it, anticipating Shakespeare).[6]

Today Camões's fame rests equally on his shorter poems; he is now considered by many, for the reasons adduced by Sena, to be "the supreme peninsular lyric poet."[7] It is important to note that in England a shift from an exclusive interest in the epic poet toward a balanced interest in both the epic and lyric poet as the basis for Camões's literary reputation began rather early. In 1687 Philip Ayres had published a translation of one of Camões's sonnets.[8] But it was William Hayley who, in the latter part of the seventeenth century, brought Camões's lyric poems to the attention of an English readership that would include Camões's earliest nineteenth-century translators. For even as he praised Mickle's translation of *Os Lusíadas*, Hayley called particular attention to Camões's sonnets, translating one of them himself and including a second, anonymous specimen. The nineteenth-century link back to Hayley was acknowledged by Lord Viscount Strangford, for instance, who made a point of thanking Hayley in the pages of his book "for the assistance of many valuable books, which could not elsewhere be procured."[9]

The subsequent stages in the rise of Camões's stock as a writer of sonnets, madrigals, and other forms of lyric poetry can be tracked. In 1803 appeared Strangford's *Poems, from the Portuguese of Luis de Camoens*. The English shift to a more balanced view of Camões as epic *and* lyric poet was well under way. Not everyone was happy with Strangford's translations. The future Poet Laureate Robert Southey, who had a strong scholarly interest in Portuguese history and literature, accused Strangford—"his Lordship"—of having "fathered his own verses upon Camoens."[10] In a lengthy two-part review of Strangford, Southey served up some of his own translations of Camões's shorter poems.

Camões the lyric poet—and often, biographically, Camões the unfortunate lover—came to the attention of other nineteenth-century English poets besides Southey, such as Wordsworth, Byron, Felicia Hemans, and, preeminently, Elizabeth Barrett, and through them their American followers including Edgar Allan Poe, Herman Melville, Thomas Wentworth Higginson, and Emily Dickinson. It is the literary history made in England, America, and Southern Africa by those poets and romancers who were at times influenced by Camões's epic and lyrical poetry that is the subject of *The Presence of Camões*. The story is one of echoes of words, images, situations, working sometimes directly from Camões (though usually in translation), but just as often through intermediary authors who, in that way, pass on the influence of Camões. I try to account for the complexity of the web of influence and appropriation by picking out some of the most significant strands. My story is not always linear. For instance, Herman Melville read William Julius Mickle's translation of *Os Lusíadas* and Lord Viscount Strangford's *Poems, from the Portuguese of Luis de Camoëns*, but he also knew Elizabeth Barrett Browning's poems that mentioned Camões, especially her widely read "Catarina to Camoëns." Edgar Allan Poe, on the other hand, suffered Camonean influences almost entirely through his knowledge of Barrett Browning's *A Drama of Exile: and other poems* (1845). Each writer discerned his own Camões and constructed his own precursor, even when the Portuguese poet's work came through refracted in the work of another poet. While they can stand alone, each chapter contributes uniquely to an overall pattern of complex literary readings and influences.

The Presence of Camões starts out by examining the ways in which Camões's contemporary, the Italian poet Torquato Tasso, has been closely linked to Camões from the start, first among the English but then in the work of the American writer Herman Melville. Subsequent chapters examine closely the ways in which Camões is present in specific works by notable English-language writers. Case studies, if you will, these chapters range in subject from the presence of Camões's Spirit of the Cape—figured as Adamastor—in the writings of the Southern African writers Roy Campbell, Charles Eglington, Douglas Livingstone, David Wright, Stephen Gray, and André Brink, to the coded uses of lines from a Camões lyric by Elizabeth Bishop. Other chapters take up William Hayley's relationship to the epic poet Joel Barlow and the English painter-poet William Blake; Elizabeth Barrett Browning's centrality in disseminating knowledge of Camões's life and poetry, especially to the American world of letters; Edgar Allan Poe's knowledge of Camões through Barrett Browning's poetry; Herman Melville's strong attraction to both Camões's epic and lyric poetry; Henry Wadsworth Longfellow's selections from Camões for his highly successful anthology *The Poets and Poetry of Europe*; Thomas Wentworth Higginson's long-standing interest in matters Portuguese with a focus on Camões; and Emily Dickinson's knowledge of Camões (like Poe's) mainly through her reading of Elizabeth Barrett Browning.

Each piece had its start in a scholarly discovery of some kind. For instance, a disinterested reading of a just-purchased copy of an early nineteenth-century edition of *Poems, from the Portuguese of Luis de Camoens* by Lord Viscount Strangford led to the discovery that the date Melville recorded in his copy of Strangford meshed with the dates of several personal and family crises. To take another example, contextualizing the lines from Camões employed by Elizabeth Bishop as the epigraph for her third volume of poems confirmed the hunch that *Questions of Travel* was intended as an ambivalent confirmation of love.

A final chapter gathers English-language translations of "the most famous verses in the Portuguese language," the lines that make up "Alma minha gentil," a poem "known to every Portuguese with the slightest pretense to education."[11] Notably, among the eighteen versions of Camões's sonnet collected (most the work of poets, ranging in date over more than two centuries) is the little-known version done by Portugal's greatest poet since Camões. It is not certain why Fernando Pessoa translated "Alma minha gentil," though it might have been intended for an anthology of Portuguese poetry in English translation that he hoped to place with an English publisher, a project that did not come off.

This study owes much to earlier scholarship. Specific debts are indicated throughout. But it is appropriate to list some of the most useful work: Félix Walter's *La Littérature Portugaise en Angleterre à L'Époque Romantique* (1927), Luis Cardim's *Projecção de Camões nas Letras Inglêsas* (1940), Carlos Augusto Gonçalves Estorninho's "O Culto de Camões em Inglaterra" (*Arquivo de Bibliografia Portuguesa*, 1961), and Madonna Letzring's *The Influence of Camoens in English Literature* (*Revista Camoniana*, 1964, 1965, and 1971). To these surveys of the uses to which English-language writers have put Camões can be added Norwood Andrews, Jr.'s *A Projecção de Camões e d'Os Lusíadas nos Estados Unidos da América* (in *Os Lusíadas: Estudos Sobre a Projecção de Camões em Culturas e Literaturas Estrangeiras*, 1984), and *Camões em Inglaterra* (1992), a collection of pieces by various hands under the direction of Maria Leonor Machado de Sousa.

1

Tasso's Legacy

Os Lusíadas was first "made English" by Sir Richard Fanshawe, a diplomat with considerable service in Spain. He brought out his translation of Camões's work in 1655. Just over a century later, in 1776, William Julius Mickle published his considerably longer version of this poem, motivated, he said, by his desire "to give a poem that might live in the English language."[1] Over time Mickle's version has proven to be the best-known of the several English translations of *Os Lusíadas*, more often reprinted than the earlier Fanshawe translation or than any succeeding version. But Fanshawe's version has had its modern adherents. In *From Virgil to Milton*, C.M. Bowra chooses to quote from Fanshawe. "No modern translator can hope to rival" the "vigour and vitality," he writes, of this translation done "when the epic was still a living art."[2] Bowra's lead was followed by Thomas R. Hart in his authoritative essay on Camões for *European Writers: The Middle Ages and the Renaissance* in 1983.[3]

Both Fanshawe and Mickle—Camões's first two English translators—chose to include in their books Torquato Tasso's encomiastic sonnet on Camões, written in 1580, along with their own translations. Tasso's "handsome tribute"—he is said to have "feared no man but Camoens"—was the first such tribute to Camões in all Europe.[4] With its appearance in Sir Richard Fanshawe's 1655 edition of his translation, it entered into the English language at the same time Camões did—both sonnet and epic being, as Fanshawe informed his readers, "now newly put into English." In *The Lusiad, or, Portugals Historicall Poem*, Fanshawe's translation of Tasso's poem appears immediately following the Italian original:

> Vasco, le cui felici adrite Antenne
> Incontro al *Sol*, che ne riporta il *giorno*,

7

Spiegar le vele, e fer colà Ritorno,
   Dove egli par che di cadere accenne:
Non più de *Te* per aspro mar sostenne
   Quel, che fece CICLOPE oltraggio, & scorno:
   Ne *chi* turbò *l'Arpie* nel suo soggiorno,
   Ne diè più bel *Subjetto* a Colte *penne.*
Et hor *quella* del colto e buon LUIGI
   Tant' oltre stende il glorioso volo
   Che i tuoi spalmati *Legni* andar men lunge.
 Ond' a *quelli*, a cui S'alza il nostro *polo*,
   Et a chi ferma incontra i suoi vestigi,
   Per *lui* del corso *tuo* la fama aggiunge.

VASCO, *whose bold and happy ships against*
   The Rising Sun (*who fraights them home with day*)
   Display'd their wings, and back again advanc't
   To where *in Seas all Night he steeps his Ray:*
Not more then Thou, *on rugged Billows felt,*
   He that bor'd out the Eye of POLYPHEME;
   Nor He *that spoyl'd the* HARPYES *where they dwelt,*
   Afforded Learned Pens *a fairer* Theam.
And this *of Learn'd and honest* CAMOENS
   So far beyond now takes it's glorious flight,
   That thy breath'd Sailes *went a less Journey, Whence*
   To Those *on whom the* Northern Pole *shines bright,*
And Those *who set* their *feet to* ours, *The boast*
Of thy Long Voyage *Travails at his Cost.*[5]

A century later Fanshawe's Elizabethan verse seemed somewhat
old-fashioned to an audience brought up on the neo-classical
translations of the ancients by masterful poets like John Dryden
and Alexander Pope. When, in his edition of *The Lusiad; or, The
Discovery of India. An Epic Poem* in 1776, William Julius Mickle
also decided to include Tasso's poem, he felt obliged to re-trans-
late Tasso's poem as well:

Vasco, whose bold and happy bowsprit bore
Against the rising morn; and, homeward fraught,
Whose sails came westward with the day, and brought
The wealth of India to thy native shore:
Ne'er did the Greek such length of seas explore;
The Greek, who sorrow to the Cyclop wrought,

And he, who, Victor, with the Harpies fought,
Never such pomp of naval honours wore.
Great as thou art, and peerless in renown,
Yet thou to Camoens ow'st thy noblest fame;
Farther than thou didst sail, his deathless song
Shall bear the dazzling splendor of thy name;
And under many a sky thy actions crown,
While Time and Fame together glide along.[6]

"Tasso never did his judgment more credit, than when he confessed that he dreaded Camoens as a rival," writes Mickle, "or his generosity more honour, than when he addressed this elegant Sonnet to the Hero of the Lusiad."[7]

But Tasso's importance to Mickle's venture in bringing *Os Lusíadas* to the attention of the English lies less in his encomium to Camões than in his having distinguished Vasco da Gama's exploits from those of Camões the poet. Whereas Fanshawe had set off Tasso's poem and his own translation of it on a discrete and separate page with no authorial comment, Mickle weaves the poem and his translation into the final pages of a long introduction. The point, of course, is that Mickle saw Gama as the single great figure of this epic of commerce (a theme that later appealed strongly to Herman Melville), choosing to play up the seafaring hero's heroic and imperialistic patriotism. The note is sounded in the opening sentence of his long introduction: "If a concatenation of events centered in one great action, events which gave birth to the present Commercial System of the World, if these be of the first importance in the civil history of mankind," he announces, "the Lusiad, of all other poems, challenges the attention of the Philosopher, the Politician, and the Gentleman."[8]

Camões's poem also had its direct practical value. It was as an employee of the East India Company that Mickle undertook his translation, a task acknowledged in his acknowledgments. "To the Gentlemen of the East India Company, who are his Subscribers," he wrote, "the Translator offers his singular thanks; and with pleasure he assures them, that their desire to see an Epic Poem, *particularly their own*, in English, greatly encouraged him in the prosecution of his laborious work."[9] His large

purpose is revealed in passages such as this one from his introduction:

> The superiority of the civil and military arts of the British, not-
> withstanding the hateful character of some individuals, is at
> this day beheld in India with all the astonishment of admira-
> tion, and all the desire of imitation. This, however retarded by
> various causes, must in time have a most important effect, must
> fulfil the prophecy of Camoens, and *transfer to the British the
> high compliment he pays to his countrymen*;
> > Beneath their sway majestic, wise and mild,
> > Proud of her victor's laws thrice happier India smiled.[10]

Even Robert Southey, who did not much like Mickle's translation, agreed with him and with Tasso in viewing "the celebrity
of Vasco da Gama" as "the work of Camoens."[11]

One cannot imagine anything being further from William
Wordsworth's mind than the benevolent cause of England's commercial empire when he undertook his translation of only part
of Tasso's sonnet on Camões. In fact, what he omits is precisely
the encomium to Vasco da Gama, thereby ignoring one of the
great forces in the annals of Portuguese discoveries that led to
an imperial Portugal. Entitled "Translation of the Sestet of a
Sonnet by Tasso," this fragment reads:

> Camoëns, he the accomplished and the good,
> Gave to thy fame a more illustrious flight
> Than that brave vessel, though she sailed so far;
> Through him her course along the Austral flood
> Is known to all beneath the polar star,
> Through him the Antipodes in thy name delight.[12]

These lines were not published in Wordsworth's lifetime. The
surviving manuscript was sold at Sotheby's in December 1896,
and the lines were first printed by Richard Garnett. To those
lines Garnett rather boldly prefixed his own translation of the
missing octave of Tasso's poem:

> Vasco, whose bold and happy mainyard spread
> Sunward thy sails where dawning glory dyed
> Heaven's orient gate; whose westering prow the tide

Clove, where the day-star bows him to his bed;
Not sterner toil than thine, or strife more dread,
Or nobler laud to nobler lyre allied—
His, who did baffled Polypheme deride,
Or his, whose soaring shaft the Harpy fled.[13]

Although there is some evidence of Wordsworth's impatience with his epic poetry, the English poet was largely an admirer of Tasso.[14] He had studied Italian with Agostino Isola, the editor of Tasso's *Gerusalemme Liberata* in 1877.[15] There are explicit allusions to Tasso in his own poetry. In *An Evening Walk* (1793), for instance, he borrows a phrase from Tasso—"dolcemente feroce," which he renders as "sweetly ferocious"—being careful to footnote his source.[16] And in *The Prelude*, while in France his thoughts run to Tasso's Erminia from *Gerusalemme Liberata* and Ariosto's Angelica from *Orlando Furioso* (Book 9, ll. 437-453). Yet when Wordsworth sets down names of illustrious writers whose work was done in exile (or prison), he fails to mention Tasso. "Dante wrote his Poem in a great measure, perhaps entirely, when exile had separated him from the passions and what he thought the social duties, of his native City," he wrote. "Cervantes, Camoens and other illustrious foreigners wrote in prison and in exile, when they were cut off from all other employments."[17] Yet he translated Chiabrera's epitaph on the Italian poet for use in an essay on epitaphs intended for Coleridge's *The Friend* but never published in his lifetime:

Torquato Tasso rests within this Tomb;
This Figure weeping from her inmost heart
Is Poesy; from such impassioned grief
Let every one conclude what this Man was.[18]

And in "Scorn not the Sonnet," his sonnet in defense of sonnets, Wordsworth again juxtaposes the names of the great Italian and Portuguese poets, as if the mention of the one necessarily evoked the other:

Scorn not the Sonnet; Critic, you have frowned,
Mindless of its just honours; with this key
Shakespeare unlocked his heart; the melody

Of this small lute gave ease to Petrarch's wound;
A thousand times this pipe did Tasso sound;
With it Camöens soothed an exile's grief;
The Sonnet glittered a gay myrtle leaf
Amid the cypress with which Dante crowned
His visionary brow: a glow-worm lamp,
It cheered mild Spenser, called from Faery-land
To struggle through dark ways; and when a damp
Fell round the path of Milton, in his hand
The Thing became a trumpet; whence he blew
Soul-animating strains—alas, too few![19]

Wordsworth's ahistorical ordering of names has been explained interestingly by John Hollander. "Clio's arrangement would start with Dante, followed by Petrarch, Camoens, Tasso, Spenser, Shakespeare, and Milton," he indicates. "That Camoens is here, and not Ronsard, Du Bellay, Giovanni della Casa (for his influence on Milton's early sonnets, for example) or Sidney, is of no concern to the Muse of history. But that the chronology is so contorted by the zigzag line of Shakespeare—Petrarch—Tasso—Camoens—Dante—Spenser—Milton must mean that it is Calliope's list and that this is indeed poetic, or nonliteral, historiography."[20] In Wordsworth, then, one has a personal history of the sonnet, one that exemplifies how writers and artists rewrite "institutional literary or art history into a visionary poetic history of their own."[21] The point here is that Wordsworth, even seeming to grant priority to Tasso, does, in fact, honor Camões's salience in what was a larger group of possible candidates, as shown in Hollander's more expansive list.

Tasso's words appear in Richard Francis Burton's two-volume translation of *Os Lusíadas* as an epigraph. The line "Bramo assai,—poco spero,—nulla chiedo" appears as one of five epigraphs to the entire work. A second line from the Italian, though unidentified—"Tu se' lo mio maestro, é lo mio autore"—appears as the epigraph to the commemorative sonnet printed on the dedication page over the initials "R.F.B." But "To My Master Camoens" is not by Burton, it appears, for his wife explains that she—Isabel Burton—wrote it, adding it to her husband's posthumously published translation. It reads:

Great Pilgrim-poet of the Sea and Land;
   Thou life-long sport of Fortune's ficklest will;
   Doomed to all human and inhuman ill,
Despite thy lover-heart, thy hero-hand:
Enrollèd by thy pen what marv'ellous band
   Of god-like Forms thy golden pages fill;
   Love, Honour, Justice, Valour, Glory thrill
The Soul, obedient to thy strong command:
Amid the Prophets highest sits the Bard,
   At once Revealer of the Heav'en and Earth,
To Heav'en the guide, of Earth the noblest guard;
And, 'mid the Poets thine the peerless worth,
   Whose glorious song, thy Genius' sole reward,
Bids all the Ages, Camoens! bless thy birth.[22]

Camões stands alone in this poem, which does not bother to mention Gama, as Tasso did. In fact, it is entirely in keeping with the romantic's turn to the poet as hero, that each of the English-language poems on Camões ignores Gama and the ostensible subject of Camões's epic. This is true of Melville, Jonathan Griffin, and Keith Bosley. Melville's poem shall be discussed in chapter 5, but suffice it to say here that the author of *Moby-Dick*, writing late in life, focuses on an infirm poet awaiting his death in the hospital. Roy Campbell was himself in hospital when he wrote his sonnet on Camões in 1943, following Burton's lead in finding in Camões a fellow poet-warrior. (Burton chose as an epigraph to his translation of *Os Lusíadas* Camões's self-characterization—"Now with the sword-hilt, then with pen in hand" ["Ora toma a espada, agora a penna"]—a line that Mickle singles out in his introduction as "One hand the pen, and one the sword employ'd.")[23]

Camões, alone, of all the lyric race,
Born in the black aurora of disaster,
Can look a common soldier in the face:
I find a comrade where I sought a master:
For daily, while the stinking crocodiles
Glide from the mangroves on the swampy shore,
He shares my awning on the dhow, he smiles,
And tells me that he lived it all before.

Through fire and shipwreck, pestilence and loss,
Led by the ignis fatuus of duty
To a dog's death—yet of his sorrows king—
He shouldered high his voluntary Cross,
Wrestled his hardships into forms of beauty,
And taught his gorgon destinies to sing.[24]

Camões as soldier reappears in Jonathan Griffin's "Camões Dying," like Melville's poem, a monologue in the sick poet's voice:

That must be all. So . . . I conclude
in absolute disappointment—glad glad
to be dying now my country's dead—this sad
end to me the one friend to me. God is good,
good: right in the middle of the vast sweep
and fast current, the punishment of a people,
He thought of a plucked poet and, for an instant,
paused; and now the pitying fingers of God
are busy unbuckling this rusty, this battered
body to discharge this thirsty, this bitter
    soul from soldiering—
                                    That's better!
                                    That's better—[25]

Griffin builds his poem around the familiar, though largely discredited, notion that Camões's death was brought on, or at least hastened, by Portugal's total subservience to Spain beginning in 1580.

Keith Bosley's untitled poem takes a different tack. It compliments Camões for what he was able to make out of his unfortunate life.

Luís de Camões
early learned the cost
of experience
with one eye's light lost

then sailed to explore
a new hemisphere
but he found it 'for
lack of stars less fair'

while his dark half sought
and brought from within
a brightness of thought
for happy the man

who from his life's wreck
swims with an epic.[26]

It was by way of Tasso, perhaps, that Camões found his first translator in the United States. Richard Henry Wilde (1789-1847), an Irish-American poet from Georgia and the author of a detailed scholarly study of Tasso, published a handful of translations of Camões's lyrics in newspapers.[27] Wilde managed to achieve some fame for his own poetry. He was best known for the poems *Hesperia* and "The Lament of the Captive" (the latter known variously as "My Life is Like the Summer Rose," "Summer Rose," and "The Complaint of the Captive"). He made a name for himself, however, as the author of *Conjectures and Researches concerning the Love, Madness, and Imprisonment of Torquato Tasso*, a two-volume work he published at his own expense in 1842. Among the book's reviewers was the poet Robert Browning, who liked it well enough to borrow hints and names surrounding the Duke of Ferrara for use in his dramatic monologue "My Last Duchess."[28]

Although *Conjectures and Researches* includes thirty or so translations from Tasso's poetry, Tasso's sonnet on Camões is not among them.[29] In fact, the Italian poet's well-known admiration for Camões goes unmentioned. Yet Wilde knew Camões's work well enough to translate and publish at least four of his sonnets. Under the pseudonym *Surrey* he published "They say the swan, though mute his whole life long" in the Augusta *Chronicle* (12 November 1821); it reappeared some time later in the *Southern Literary Messenger* (December 1834), with Wilde this time identified as translator.[30] A truncated version of the same poem—lines 1-2 and 5-7—appeared on 29 January 1835 in the Pittsfield *Sun*, which identifies it as "Sonnet xliii of the edition of 1779-1780."[31] Of Wilde's three other translations from Camões—"My years were short and troubled upon earth," "To thee sunny isle in this ocean of life," and "Flow on silver stream to the Ocean!"—it is not known whether any or all achieved print during his lifetime.

Before deciding to publish his book on Tasso himself, Wilde enlisted the aid of several of his contemporaries in the search for a publisher. Among those who tried unsuccessfully to aid him in the matter was Henry Wadsworth Longfellow. The well-known Harvard University professor was already at work on an anthology of the *Poets and Poetry of Europe*. The compilation, conceived and executed on a grand scale, appeared in 1845, just two years before Wilde's death. Wilde is represented in the book, in the section on Italian poetry, with eighteen examples— one *canzone* and seventeen sonnets—of his translations of Tasso.[32] But none of his translations appear in the section devoted to Camões. For examples of Camões's lyrics, Longfellow turned, rather, to the British, to the work of Felicia Hemans, Lord Viscount Strangford, and Thomas Roscoe. In Roscoe's case he included his version of "No mundo poucos anos, e cansados," which Wilde and Strangford had also translated. Longfellow chose other examples of Camões's work in Strangford's translations, but not Wilde's. Possibly, Longfellow's failure to include Wilde's work on Camões in *Poets and Poetry of Europe* signifies only that he did not know that it existed.[33]

2

William Hayley's Patronage

William Hayley's importance in the story of Camões in England and the United States is tripartite: he commissioned the first portrait of Camões done in England; his *Essay on Epic Poetry* directed an American poet to William Julius Mickle's translation of *Os Lusíadas*; and while greatly admiring Camões's epic, he took the lead in calling attention to Camões's achievement as a lyric poet.

The entry on William Hayley in S. Foster Damon's *A Blake Dictionary* begins: "HAYLEY (William, 1745-1820), poet, biographer, connoisseur, and patron, is remembered today chiefly as the man who persuaded Blake to live near him at Felpham (1800-1803); and Blake's stinging epigrams have done much to ruin his would-be friend's reputation."[1]

Posterity has not been kind to Hayley, whose literary and artistic pretensions seem to have far exceeded his talents and outstripped his achievements. In *English Bards and Scotch Reviewers*, Byron took his measure in calling attention to "HAYLEY'S last work and worst—until his next" (line 310).[2] In 1982 David Bindham writes, "Hayley was a country gentleman of some literary reputation, who turned out an endless stream of vapid verse."[3]

Yet he has also had his defenders. In his time—Byron notwithstanding—Hayley was designated, in Robert Southey's words (repeated by Thomas Wentworth Higginson), "'by popular election the king of the English poets;' and he was held so important a personage, that he received, what probably no other author ever has won, a large income for the last twelve years of his life in return for the prospective copyright of his posthumous memoirs."[4] "But," continues Higginson, writing in the lat-

ter part of the nineteenth century, "probably nine out of ten
who shall read these lines will have to consult a biographical
dictionary to find out who Hayley was; while his odd *protégé*,
William Blake, whom the fine ladies of the day wondered at
Hayley for patronizing, has since become a favorite in literature and art."[5] A century later no one would remember Hayley's
name were it not for its association with that of William Blake.

For some three years—1800-1803—Hayley did in fact support Blake, "the impecunious engraver," with commissions.[6]
Hayley thought the arrangement agreeable to both parties,
though Blake apparently did feel somewhat cut off from his
former London life and the interests he had left behind. In 1803
"the kind indefatigable Blake," was still begging "a little fresh
news from the spiritual world," wrote Hayley to a friend who
might supply such news.[7]

Upon Blake's arrival in 1800, John Flaxman, a mutual friend,
had written to William Hayley: "I hope that Blake's residence
at Felpham will be a Mutual Comfort to you & him, & I see no
reason why he should not make as good a livelihood there as
in London, if he engraves & teaches drawing, by which he may
gain considerably as also by making neat drawings of different
kinds," he wrote, continuing on to warn, "but if he places any
dependence on painting large pictures, for which he is not quali-
fied, either by habit or study, he will be miserably deceived."[8]
Hayley must have agreed, for during "the spring of 1801," according to G.E. Bentley, "Blake was apparently kept busy making miniatures for Hayley."[9] But Hayley also commissioned from
the "good enthusiastic" and indefatigable Blake a series of portraits of poets, twenty heads intended as adornments to Hayley's
library at Marine Turret, Felpham, Sussex. When finished, "the
canvasses range[d] in width from 19" to 41"," "their height"—
"almost uniform"—"not exceed[ing] 16 1/2"."[10] Originally, Blake
was to paint portraits of William Cowper, Spenser, Cowley,
Cicero, Voltaire, Shakespeare, Dryden, Sappho, Tasso, Camoens,
Anacreon, Pope, Euripides, Ariosto, Demosthenes, Homer, Livy,
and Gibbon. Soon, it appears, Anacreon was replaced by Ercilla,
and Livy by Horace. Ultimately, Blake made eighteen portraits,
the subjects of which are Cowper, Spenser, Chaucer, Cicero,
Voltaire, Shakespeare, Dryden, Milton, Tasso, Camoens, Ercilla,

William Blake's portrait of Camões.

Pope, Otway, Dante, Demosthenes, Homer, Klopstock, and Thomas Alphonso Hayley (Hayley's son, recently dead at the age of
twenty).[11]

As early as 26 November 1800, Blake reported to his patron
that he was "absorbed by the poets Milton, Homer, Camoens,
Ercilla, Ariosto, and Spenser, whose physiognomies have been
my delightful study. . . ."[12] Ultimately, "twenty heads with appropriate attributes were painted in tempera on separate can-
vases."[13] To Alexander Gilchrist's *Life of William Blake* (1863),
W.M. Rossetti contributed "Annotated Lists of Blake's Paintings,
Drawings, and Engravings." Rossetti's annotations were repeated in the Blake Society volume of reproductions. In *Notes
and Queries* in 1926, under the title "Blake's 'Heads of the Poets,'" appeared K. Povey's series of "notes correct[ing] and
supplement[ing] some of Rossetti's identifications and descriptions."[14]

Povey's commentary on Blake's "Camoens" is informative:
"The accessory, an anchor, is the device of Cape Colony, an al-

lusion to the episode in the 'Lusiads' of Vasco da Gama's rounding the Cape of Good Hope. Or perhaps it refers more generally to his voyage to the Indies." So far so good. Then Povey writes: "It is curious that Camoens is represented as blind in the left eye instead of in the right, as he was in reality."[15] Indeed, if this is so, it is a curiosity, but the error is not unprecedented in English texts relating to Camões and his work. Naturally Blake's painting of Camões was based on some source almost certainly supplied by Hayley, who must have been the Felpham's most fervid—if not only—reader of Camões. Before conjecturing on which earlier portrait or illustration Blake might have copied from, and since we know that Blake was not much of a student of Camões's work, it might be useful to consider what is known about Hayley's knowledge of Camões.

In 1782 William Hayley published *An Essay on Epic Poetry; in Five Epistles*. In the "Third Epistle" he took up, in addition to a "Sketch of the Northern and the Provençal Poetry," the "most distinguished Epic Poets of Italy, Spain, Portugal, France, and England." Camões's *Os Lusíadas* he praised in the highest terms, pointing directly to the William Julius Mickle translation published just six years earlier, in 1776. Surprisingly, William Hayley's name does not appear in the list of subscribers to Mickle's translation, an extensive list that, besides including the names of Oliver Goldsmith and David Garrick (who was down for twenty copies), bears those of James Boswell and Samuel Johnson. Johnson, who translated (from the French) Father Jerome Lobo's *A Voyage to Abyssinia*, asserted that at one time he had himself considered translating *Os Lusíadas*.[16] The absence of Hayley's name from the subscriber's list for Mickle's work suggests that he probably did not know Camões's work until he read Mickle's translation. Indeed, his comment in his *Essay on Epic Poetry* fails to acknowledge the fact that *Os Lusíadas* had been translated into English first by Sir Richard Fanshawe in 1655 or that it had been praised by Voltaire in *An Essay on Epick Poetry*, written in English and published in London in 1727 while the Frenchman was in exile in England.[17]

> Tho' fiercest tribes her galling fetters drag,
> Proud Spain must strike to Lusitania's flag,
> Whose ampler folds, in conscious triumph spread,

Wave o'er her NAVAL POET's laureate head.
Ye Nymphs of Tagus, from your golden cell,
That caught the echo of his tuneful shell,
Rise, and to deck your darling's shrine provide
The richest treasures that the deep may hide;
From every land let grateful Commerce shower
Her tribute to the Bard who sung her power;
As those rich gales, from whence his GAMA caught
A pleasing earnest of the prize he sought,
The balmy fragrance of the East dispense,
So steals his Song on the delighted sense,
Astonishing, with sweets unknown before,
Those who ne'er tasted but of classic lore.
Immortal Bard, thy name with GAMA vies,
Thou, like thy Hero, with propitious skies
The sail of bold adventure hast unfurl'd,
And in the Epic ocean found a world.
'Twas thine to blend the Eagle and the Dove,
At once the Bard of Glory and of Love:
Thy thankless Country heard thy varying lyre
To PETRARCH's Softness melt, and swell to HOMER's Fire!
Boast and lament, ungrateful land, a Name,
In life, in death, thy honor and thy shame.[18]

It is in glossing the line "At once the Bard of Glory and of Love"
that Hayley calls attention to Camões as a lyric poet (also briefly
mentioned in Mickle's introduction)[19] whose work in that vein
was still, in 1782, virtually unknown in England:

The Epic powers of Camoens have received their due honour in
our language, by the elegant and spirited translation of Mr.
Mickle; but our country is still a stranger to the lighter graces
and pathetic sweetness of his shorter compositions. These, as
they are illustrated by the Spanish notes of his indefatigable Com-
mentator, *Manuel de Faria*, amount to two volumes in folio. I
shall present the reader with a specimen of his Sonnets, for which
he is celebrated as the rival of Petrarch. Of the three translations
which follow, I am indebted for the two first to an ingenious
friend, from whom the public may with me to have received more
extensive obligations of a similar nature. It may be proper to add,
that the first Sonnet of Camoens, like that of Petrarch, is a kind
of preface to the amorous poetry of its author.[20]

Hayley's insistence on the importance and high quality of Camões's lyrics initiated the English Romantics' interest in Camões's sonnets and songs, as well as the life they seemed to document. In this respect, one can draw a line from Hayley to Lord Viscount Strangford, whose 1803 collection of *Poems, from the Portuguese of Luis de Camoens*, introduced by his biographically fanciful essay, "Remarks on the Life and Writings of Camoens," sparked the interest in Camões and his lyric poetry of such other poets as William Lisle Bowles, John Cam Hobhouse, Robert Dunbar, Lord Byron, and Elizabeth Barrett Browning—all of whom wrote poems on Camões and Camonean themes. Strangford seems to acknowledge William Hayley's primacy by singling him out.[21] In "Notes to the Third Epistle," Hayley had also provided, along with their originals, three of Camões's sonnets—"While on my head kind Fortune deign'd to pour" ("Em quanto quis Fortuna que tivesse"), "Go, gentle spirit! now supremely blest" ("Alma minha gentil, que te partiste"), and "While prest with woes from which it cannot flee" ("Quando de minhas magoas a comprida")—in English translation.[22] He did not go so far as later students of Camões would go in giving primacy to the lyric impulse in Camões over that of the epic. In the twentieth century Aubrey Bell, for example, said flatly that "although to a Portuguese Camões must ever be the author of the *Lusiads*, to the lover of poetry he is first and foremost a great lyric poet"; but Hayley was the first critic in England to call attention to the worth of Camões's "shorter" productions.[23]

When Blake needed a portrait of Camões to work from as he toiled on the "Heads of the Poets" for the new library at Turret, Mickle's volume proved to be no help, for Camões's portrait does not appear in the 1776 edition. In *Memoirs of the Life and Writings of Luis de Camoens* (1820), however, John Adamson offers us the clue to Blake's source. He writes: "so careless have certain artists been, that in prints in Faria e Sousa's Commentary on the Lusiad, and in Sir Richard Fanshaw's translation of that poem, Camoens appears blind of the wrong eye, from the plate having been reversed, a liberty too frequently taken by engravers."[24] What is most likely is that Blake worked either from a copy of Fanshawe's 1655 translation or from a copy of

Frontispiece to Sir Richard Fanshawe's 1655 *Lusiad.*

Faria e Sousa's commentary—a work Hayley mentions in his *Essay on Epic Poetry* and one which contains the picture of Camões that is obviously the source for the frontispiece in Fanshawe's 1655 translation. Apparently neither Blake, who could hardly be called a student of Camões's work, nor Hayley, who purported to be both a student and a warm admirer of the Portuguese poet, caught the mistake in this portrait of Camões.[25]

Several years before engaging Blake to paint the portraits, including Camões's, that would adorn his library, Hayley introduced Camões's epic to Joel Barlow. In 1786 the American poet visited Hayley and at the time gave him a copy of an unpublished poem. Hayley commented on *The Vision of Columbus*, but not until 1792, six years after Barlow's visit. His principal suggestion, that Barlow compress his poem, fell on deaf ears. But the call for a contemporary epic poem that he made in *An Essay on Epic Poetry* did not. "Hayley had nowhere provided Barlow specific guidelines toward compressing his poem into an epic," notes John McWilliams, "but the direction of Hayley's 'Essay' was tonic indeed."[26] It took Barlow years, but by 1807 he had transformed his poem in the form of Columbus's prison "vision" into *The Columbiad*, the epic-narrative he spun out of the mariner's soliloquy.[27]

In Hayley's "Essay on Epic Poetry" Barlow had also read of the existence of William Julius Mickle's translation of *Os*

Lusíadas (1776). Like *Os Lusíadas*, *The Columbiad* tells a tale
of maritime discovery and empire. Mickle's translation had its
effect on Barlow's more ambitious try at the epic, even in some
of the poem's particulars such as the portrayal of Atlas, whom
Barlow considers "as the guardian Genius of Africa."[28] His description of the giant he calls Atlas seems to owe a good deal to
Mickle's English rendering of Camões's Adamastor:

> Hark! a dread voice, with heaven-astounding strain,
> Swells like a thousand thunders o'er the main,
> Rolls and reverberates around thy hills,
> And Hesper's heart with pangs paternal fills.
> Thou hearst him not; tis Atlas, throned sublime,
> Great brother guardian of old Afric's clime;
> High o'er his coast he rears his frowning form,
> O'erlooks and calms his sky-borne fields of storm,
> Flings off the clouds that round his shoulders hung,
> And breaks from clogs of ice his trembling tongue;
> While far thro space with rage and grief he glares,
> Heaves his hoar head and shakes the heaven he bears[.][29]

Mickle's lines read:

> I spoke, when rising through the darken'd air,
> Appall'd we saw an hideous Phantom glare;
> High and enormous o'er the flood he tower'd,
> And thwart our way with sullen aspect lour'd:
> An earthy paleness o'er his cheeks was spread,
> Erect uprose his hairs of wither'd red;
> Writhing to speak his sable lips disclose,
> Sharp and disjoin'd, his gnashing teeth's blue rows;
> His haggard beard flow'd quivering on the wind,
> Revenge and horror in his mien combined;
> His clouded front, by withering lightnings scared,
> The inward anguish of his soul declared.
> His red eyes glowing from their dusky caves
> Shot livid fires: Far ecchoing o'er the waves
> His voice resounded, as the cavern'd shore
> With hollow groan repeats the tempest's roar,
> Cold gliding horrors thrill'd each hero's breast,
> Our bristling hairs and tottering knees confest

Wild dread, the while with visage ghastly wan,
His black lips trembling, thus the fiend began[.][30]

Although both Camões's Adamastor and Barlow's Atlas share a classical genealogy,[31] it is notable that Camões's Eurocentric view of Adamastor as monster is at odds with Barlow's Amerocentric view of Atlas as the guardian of Africa who laments the enslavement of the Afric people, beginning with an account of the crimes Americans have committed against Africans.[32] Interestingly, as will be seen in a later chapter, Barlow's Atlas is re-invented in the rehistoricized Adamastor of contemporary Southern African writing, especially in recent work such as André Brink's *Cape of Storms*.

3

Elizabeth Barrett's
Central Poem

There is not much modern commentary on Elizabeth Barrett's poem "Catarina to Camoëns." Its reputation seems long ago to have fallen to a very low estate.[1] Indeed, it is exceedingly difficult for anyone, a century and a half after the poem's first publication in *Graham's Magazine* in 1843, to argue with great conviction for its intrinsic worth. Yet this poem of 152 lines— nineteen stanzas of eight lines each—in which the lovely and loved lady, who would die during the absence of the poet, "is supposed to muse thus while dying," merits something more than the silence to which it has fallen heir.

Throughout the nineteenth century "Catarina to Camoëns" remained one of Elizabeth Barrett's best-known poems.[2] It was particularly favored, it seems, by poets. The recluse poet Emily Dickinson, for instance, an ardent follower of Mrs. Browning, knew the "Catarina" poem well enough to quote from it in a letter to a knowing correspondent. To Mrs. J.G. Holland, the wife of the poet-novelist who doubled as editor of the *Century* magazine, she could write, "I hope I have not tired 'Sweetest Eyes were ever seen,'" and, several years later, to the same friend (referring to the Hollands' daughter), "for Katrina's Eyes, Camoens is sorry." The reference, in both cases, is to the refrain employed by Elizabeth Browning: "Sweetest eyes, were ever seen."[3] It was the refrain as well that Herman Melville recognized when he came across Browning's source, Lord Viscount Strangford's loose translation of Camões's own quite different poem about his lover's eyes. In his copy of Strangford's edition of *Poems, from the Portuguese of Luis de Camoens*, Melville triple-checked the poem beginning "The heart that warm'd my guileless breast" and then he underlined all but the first word of the refrain "And sweetest eyes that e'er were seen!"—adding at the bottom of the page the note: "Mrs Browning's verses on this."[4] That Melville would allude to Elizabeth Browning's "Catarina to Camoëns" when reading translations of Camões's lyric poems is especially noteworthy, given the importance of Camões's work, especially his epic *Os Lusíadas*, to Melville's own extensive sea novels, including, above all, *Moby-Dick*.

There were those who unequivocally considered "Catarina to Camoëns" the poet's finest achievement. John Ruskin, for one, waxed enthusiastically over the poem. To his friend Mary Russell Mitford he wrote on 22 April 1854 that he had had a "feast" that Sunday morning, reading her "dear friend's poems—Elizabeth Browning." "I have not had my eyes so often wet for these five years," he added; "I had no conception of her power before. I can't tell you how wonderful I think them." Among the half dozen of her poems he would single out was her "Catarina to Camoëns."[5] A year later, to Elizabeth Browning herself, Ruskin would praise the poem even further. On 6 April he wrote that among the various schemes he had then in hand was "the endeavour to revive the art of Illumination." And to that end he had, "the day before yesterday," made his "best work-man . . . copy out the beginning of the Catarina to Camoens," which poem was, "on the whole"—he remarked—"my favourite." He had rejected "a canto of Dante" in favor of Elizabeth Browning's poem, and he expected the result to become "one of the most glorious little burning books that ever had leaf turned by white finger." "I shall put one stanza in each vellum page," he promised, "with deep blue and purple and golden embroider."[6] On 2 June, from Florence, Elizabeth Browning answered gratefully: "My husband is very much pleased, and particularly pleased that you selected 'Catarina,' which is his favourite among my poems for some personal fanciful reasons besides the rest."[7]

The words, "besides the rest," one can assume, refer to the intrinsic merit of the poem; just as the phrase, "for some personal fanciful reasons," refers to the personal, sentimental value the poem had for Browning himself. He had been "greatly impressed" with the poem, having been affected "to tears, . . . again and again," even before he "became personally acquainted with [its] writer whose condition in certain respects had, at one time or so I fancied, resembled those of the Portuguese Caterina," as he would reveal some time after Elizabeth's death in 1861.[8] So close had he fancied the relationship between the invalid poet and the dying Catarina that in his letters to her during their courtship in 1845-1846, he could not help sprinkling about allusions to, and echoes of, his favorite poem. Did her efforts to answer his letters stay the production of "more Berthas and Caterinas and Geraldines, more great and beautiful poems of which [he] shall be—how proud!" he would be consumed with worry.[9] Yet his volume *Bells & Pomegranates* "has succeeded beyond my most adventurous wishes in one respect," he wrote gallantly. "'Blessed eyes mine eyes have been, if—' [playing on "Catarina's" refrain as he would do several times] if there was any sweetness in the tongue or flavour in the seeds to *her.*"[10] Fears that he would lose Elizabeth caused him to see the whole of the threat, to "*apprehend,* comprehend entirely, for the first time . . . the whole sense of that *closed door* of Catarina's . . .," he wrote; "and it was *I* who said—not as quoting or adapting another's words, but spontaneously, unavoidably, '*In that door, you will not enter, I have*'. . . . And, dearest, the Unwritten it must remain."[11] Again Browning alludes to "Catarina to Camoëns," this time to the opening:

> On the door you will not enter,
>   I have gazed too long—adieu!
> Hope withdraws her peradventure—
>   Death is near me,—and not *you!*[12]

At other moments he would ring the changes of a phrase Elizabeth had used in the second stanza: "In heart-playing." Insisting to Elizabeth, "as I may have told you once,—as I tell myself always—you are *entirely* what I love," and that "all about you is 'to my heart'," he would further insist that he knew "*when* to have done with fancyings and merely flitting permissible 'inly-sayings with heart-playing.'"[13] When, in less than a month, he playfully alluded again to the same stanza, he promised never again to parody her verses so.[14] But he was soon back at it, asking tentatively, "May I say 'in heart-playing'"?[15] Three months later, he would recall the third stanza to make a point regarding their then distant future. "My two letters!" he exclaimed. "I think we must institute solemn days whereon such letters are to be read years hence . . when shall I ask you,—(all being known, many weaknesses you do not choose to see now, and perhaps some strength and constancy you cannot be sure of) . . (for the charm may break, you think) . . [and here he resorts to lines from "Catarina to Camoëns"] 'if you stood *there'* . . at Wimpole St. in the room . . would you whisper 'Love, I love you, as before?' Oh, how fortunately, fortunately the next verse comes with its sweetest reassurance!"[16] The next verse—the sweetly reassuring verse that he felt no need to quote—answers the question fervidly:

> Yes! I think, were you besides them,
>   Near the bed I die upon,—
> Though their beauty you denied them,
>   As you stood there looking down.
>   You would truly
>   Call them duly,
> For the love's sake found therein,—
> 'Sweetest eyes, were ever seen.'[17]

The practical purpose of these allusions and quotations is not at all elusive. Having discerned that "Catarina to Camoëns" dramatized a keening voice with meaning deeply private to the retiring poet on Wimpole Street, Browning had hit on the happy notion (for him) of turning the poem back on the poet, doing it again and again, to assure her that the equation between herself and Catarina and that between her suitor and Catarina's, though tantalizingly close, were not entirely exact. Browning would enact the happy denouement that had eluded Camões. In her sickroom Elizabeth need not muse about an exiled lover, as had Catarina on her deathbed—even though she could well imagine the poignancy of an unfulfilled love were Robert's suit, for whatever reason, to fail at the very moment that she could foresee the possibility of the eleventh-hour return of her suitor, a happy fate that had been denied Catarina and Camões.

That the calculations—unconscious or otherwise—of Elizabeth's lover were unerring is attested to in still another way: he could count on having his every action away from her reported to her directly. With thrilled pleasure she wrote to him on 12 May 1846 after having heard a report from Mrs. Jameson: "how you had recited 'in a voice & manner as good as singing,' my 'Catarina.' How are such things to be borne, do you think, when people are not made of marble?" she asked. "But I took a long breath, & held my mask on with both hands."[18] At the moment of reading this—it is difficult not to think—Browning must have felt deep gratitude to Mrs. Jameson, not to mention Camões. A month later Browning's suit would end successfully when, in a private ceremony culminating that most romantic of all Victorian courtships, his "Portuguese Catarina" became his wife.

The poem's importance to Robert and Elizabeth did not cease with their dramatic wedding. Three years later Elizabeth showed her husband a sheaf of sonnets she had written about him as suitor and lover. Since she had withheld the poems because she had heard from him "some mistaken word" against "putting one's loves into verses," Browning would later insist, the two of them had entered into the subterfuge of publishing the group of poems under the "purposely . . . ambiguous title," *Sonnets from the Portuguese.*[19] They hoped, apparently, that readers of her *Poems* in 1850 would be so "little versed in Portuguese literature" that they would take the title to mean "Sonnets . . . *from the Portuguese language.*" If so, they would fail to detect the nature of what were highly personal love poems. In reality the title referred to the Portuguese "Catarina," wrote Browning, who left Camões "the riband from her hair."[20] In Elizabeth's poem Catarina's gift to her departing suitor is the subject of the sixteenth stanza:

> Keep my riband! take and keep it,—
> I have loosed it from my hair;
> Feeling, while you overweep it,
> Not alone in your despair,—
> Since with saintly
> Watch, unfaintly,

Out of Heaven shall o'er you lean
'Sweetest eyes, were ever seen.'[21]

The collection of "Sonnets from the Portuguese" was favorably
received, although not all its reviewers recognized that the lyrics expressed the poet's own love. But neither were they convinced that the poems were simply translations. The writer in
Fraser's Magazine saw that whatever they were, they were at
least something more than that. "From the Portuguese they may
be," he wrote, "but their life and earnestness must prove Mrs.
Browning either to be the most perfect of all known translators, or to have quickened with her own spirit the framework
of another's thoughts, and then modestly declined the honour
which was really her own."[22] If "Sonnets from the Portuguese"
do not derive from Portuguese originals, it should nevertheless
be noted that the title the Brownings settled on for Elizabeth's
sheaf of sonnets does echo Lord Strangford's title for his translations—*Poems, from the Portuguese of Luis de Camoens*.

"Catarina to Camoëns" clearly does derive from Camões,
though not directly, for Elizabeth Barrett Browning—though
trained in the classical languages—had neither Portuguese nor
Spanish, the two languages in which Camões wrote his poetry.[23]
Camões's work had been known in English translation, as early
as 1655, with Fanshawe's spirited version of Camões's epic of
discovery and empire, but in 1803 English readers were introduced in proper fashion to a different Camões—not the poet of
his country's heroic past but the poet of courtly lyrics and songs
of exile. In that year Strangford published his modest collection of *Poems*. As important to Camões's English reputation as
the poems themselves was Strangford's thirty-three pages of
introductory "Remarks on the Life and Writings of Camoens."
It was those "remarks" on Camões's "romantic" life that created the climate in which the poems themselves would appeal
to English readers. And more. To a considerable extent it was
the Camões of Strangford's *Poems*, concludes one student, "as
much as the poems of Camoens" that "brought 'admiration and
applause' from Strangford's readers, their romantic spirit finding nourishment in the tragic story of the unappreciated poet,
exiled because of his unfortunate love for Caterina de Ataide,

and, reduced to penury in his last days, sustained only by what his loyal servant could beg for them."[24] Strangford, it is true, had not been the first of the English translators to note the romantic vicissitudes of Camões's life; Mickle, over a quarter of a century earlier, had already done so. "But it was to these aspects of the poet's life," writes Strangford's critic, "that Strangford gave almost exclusive attention in his biography and notes." And he did even more. "Likewise, it was those lyrics chosen primarily for their supposedly autobiographical erotic or melancholy content, and thus contributing to the total picture of the poet himself, that most attracted readers of the nineteenth century. In addition, his final neglect and impoverishment as well as his misfortunes in love gave such poets as William Lisle Bowles and Elizabeth Barrett Browning subject matter for their own poems."[25]

Later it will be useful to consider Strangford's account of Camões's chivalric love for Catarina. But first, let us look at a Portuguese text not by Camões that might have influenced Browning both directly and by way of its impact on Strangford. *Letters of a Portuguese Nun* was first published in French in 1669 as *Lettres d'une Religieuse Portugaise* and widely re-published in several languages throughout Europe over the next two centuries. As early as 1678 it had made its way into English.[26] Composed of five letters written by a woman, this little book purported to be a French translation of Portuguese originals. Their documentary authenticity as the record of an ill-starred affair of love, seduction, and abandonment between a flesh-and-blood Portuguese nun at Beja—Mariana Alcoforado—and an historically verifiable French army officer—Noël Bouton de Chamilly—has been often questioned.[27] Jean Jacques Rousseau, whose *La nouvelle Héloise* (1761) can be seen as belonging in some ways to the same genre of epistolary fiction, thought *Lettres* the work of a male, but the general reader into the twentieth century has taken at pretty much face value the original publisher's claim that the documents are the work of a Portuguese religious unhappy in love. A standard mid-nineteenth-century reference work reflects the average reader's understanding of the work: "*Portuguese Nun*. Mariana Alcoforada [*sic*] (d. about 1700), a Portuguese lady who addressed a series of famous letters to the Chevalier de Chamilly, with whom she was deeply in love, though he did not reciprocate her passion. She derived the sobriquet from her supposed connection with a convent."[28]

Roger L'Estrange, who provided the first English version of the *Lettres* in 1678, addressed his reader:

> You are to take this Translation very Kindly, for the Author of it has ventur'd his Reputation to Oblige you: Ventur'd it (I say) even in the very Attempt of Copying so Nice an Original. It is, in *French*, one of the most Artificial Pieces perhaps of the kind, that is any where Extant: Beside the Peculiar Graces, and Felicities of that Language, in the Matter of an *Amour*, which cannot be adopted into any other Tongue without Extream Force, and Affectation. There was (it seems) an *Intrigue* of Love carry'd on betwixt a *French Officer*, and a *Nun* in Portugal. The Cavalier forsakes his Mistress, and Returnes for *France*. The Lady expostulates the Business in five Letters of Complaint, which She sends after him; and those five Letters are here at your Service. You will find in them the Lively Image of an Extravagant, and an Unfortunate Passion; and that *a Woman may be Flesh and Bloud*, in a Cloyster, as well as in a Palace.[29]

L'Estrange's hedge—"it seems"—already introduces an element of doubt as to whether these letters are authentic. But fact or fiction, as a love story with familiarly unfortunate consequences and a painful end, *Letters of a Portuguese Nun* soon earned for itself a lasting place in Western sentimental literature. The *Letters* had an immediate and immense effect. First of all the work gave English letter-writing "a new direction," asserts one student.

> These letters of a Portuguese nun to a French cavalier revealed to our [English] writers how a correspondence might be managed to unfold a simple story. Edition after edition of the *Portuguese Letters* followed, and fictitious replies and counter replies. In the wake of these continuations the *Letters of Heloise and Abelard* were translated into English, containing a similar but more pathetic tale. They, too, went through many editions,

and were imitated, mutilated and trivialized. As a result of this fashion of letter writing, there existed in the eighteenth century a considerable body of short stories in letter form.[30]

Beyond its effect on the short story, the *Lettres portugaises* gave impetus to the rise of the English novel in epistolary form, for beginning with its publication "the letter had been recognized as the true voice of feeling."[31] A line runs from *Lettres portugaises* to Samuel Richardson's epistolary novels *Pamela* (1740-1741) and *Clarissa* (1747-48)—each a "female novel of love."[32] In fact, a latter-day English translator of the *Lettres* affirms that "they have provided a generic name ["Portuguese"], notably used by Elizabeth Barrett Browning, for that kind of literature which unmasks the naked emotions of the human heart in love."[33]

Not surprisingly, Mariana Alcoforado figures in the poetry of Elizabeth Barrett Browning. *Letters* has its own relationship to "Catarina to Camoëns."[34] Since Browning was aware that any letters Catarina de Ataide might have written to Luis de Camões (if any) were no longer extant, she found herself free to invent and tell the narrative of Catarina's last days in her own voice. Such hints as she found in *Letters of a Portuguese Nun* she added to those from her main source, Strangford's *Poems, from the Portuguese of Luis de Camoens* (1803), which itself owes something to Mariana Alcoforado's letters.

Much of Elizabeth Barrett Browning's knowledge about Camões's life and the refrain she would make famous in her poem—"Sweetest eyes that e'er were seen"—can be traced to Strangford's introduction and, particularly, to his rather loose translation of one of Camões's Spanish poems:

> The heart that warm'd my guileless breast
>   Some wanton hand had thence convey'd,
> But Love, who saw his bard distress'd,
>   In pity thus the thief betray'd—
> "'Tis she who owns the fairest mien
> And sweetest eyes that e'er were seen!"
>
> And sure if Love be in the right,
>   (And was Love ever in the wrong?)
> To thee, my first and sole delight,

> That simple heart must now belong—
> —Because thou hast the fairest mien
> And sweetest eyes that e'er were seen![35]

Line six, repeated as line twelve, became the refrain of her nineteen-stanza poem.

The love portrayed in "Catarina to Camoëns" is chivalric. Strangford, drawing largely upon a strictly autobiographical interpretation of Camões's sonnets and songs, writes:

> Love is very nearly allied to devotion, and it was in the exercise of the latter that Camoens was introduced to the knowledge of the former. In the Church of "Christ's Wounds," at Lisbon, on the 11th of April, 1542, he first beheld Dona Caterina de Ataide, the object of his purest and earliest attachment. The churches of Spain and Portugal, says Scarron, are the very cradles of intrigue, and it was not long before Camoens enjoyed an opportunity of declaring his affection, with all the romantic ardour of eighteen, and of a poet.
>
> But, in those days, love was a state of no trifling probation, and ladies then unconscionably expected a period of almost chivalrous servitude, which, happily for gentlemen, is no longer required. The punctilious severity of his mistress formed the subject of our poet's most tender complaints; for, though her heart had secretly decided in his favour, still Portuguese delicacy suppressed all avowal of her passion. After many months of adoration, when he humbly besought a ringlet of her hair, she was so far softened by his entreaties, as to make a compromise with prudery, and bestow one of the silken fillets which encircled her head. . . .
>
> The peculiar situation of Dona Caterina (that of one of the queen's ladies) imposed an uniform restraint on her lover, which soon became intolerable. Like another Ovid, he violated the sanctity of the royal precincts, and was in consequence banished from the court. . . . On the morning of his departure, his mistress relented from her wonted severity, and confessed the secret of her long-concealed affection. The sighs of grief were soon lost in those of mutual delight, and the hour of parting was, perhaps, the sweetest of our poet's existence.[36]

It was at this time, it is reputed, that Camões obtained permission to accompany his King to Africa in an expedition against the Moors. There he participated in several battles, suffering, in one of them, the loss of an eye. His heroic conduct, Strangford notes,

> . . . at length purchased his recal to court. He hastened home, fraught with the most tender anticipations, and found—what must have been his feelings? that his mistress was no more!—
>   There can scarcely be conceived a more interesting theme for the visions of romance, than the death of this young and amiable being. The circumstances of her fate are peculiarly favourable to the exercise of conjecture. She loved, she was beloved, yet unfortunate in her attachment, she was torn from the world at the early age of twenty; and we cannot but adorn her grave with some of the wildest flowers which fancy produces.[37]

Other English poets, before Elizabeth Browning, had tried their hand at poems fancying the details of Camões's loves and life. In the seventeenth century, in *Lyric Poems, Made in Imitation of the Italians, Of which many are Translations from other Languages* (1687), Philip Ayres offered one example of Camões as a lyric poet, and a century later, in his *An Essay on Epic Poetry* (1782), William Hayley recognized Camões as a lyric poet as well as the author of one of the Western world's premier epics. Hayley was followed by Thomas Russel, who in *Sonnets and Miscellaneous Poems* (1789) published translations of two of Camões's sonnets.[38] But it was the appearance of Strangford's translations in 1803 that made English poets cognizant of the details, documented and made-up, of Camões's difficult life. In "Stanzas to a Lady, With the Poems of Camoens" (1807), for example, Lord Byron paid handsome tribute to the Portuguese bard; while in his "Last Song of Camoens," William Lisle Bowles drew upon, and modified, Strangford's account of Camões's penury in his last days. Felicia Dorothea Hemans, in 1818, published anonymously her own skillful collection of *Translations from Camoens and Other Poets*,[39] and Wordsworth, in 1827, called upon Camões as a distinguished practitioner in his poem "Scorn not the Sonnet." Even Elizabeth Barrett's poem on Catarina's love for Camões was anticipated in England. John

Cam Hobhouse, Byron's friend, had written in 1804 of Camões's fateful love for Catarina de Ataide. Strangford's account, as Hobhouse acknowledges, lies behind his poem:

> Accept what youth to matchless beauty gives;
> Here Camoens' soul in Strangford's numbers lives,
> A soul how vigorous, and how skill'd to move
> All other breasts, a slave alone to love.[40]

It is interesting to note that these lines come actually from a short dedicatory poem, "Verses Written in Lord Strangford's Translation of Camoens and presented to a young lady who was going to Lisbon for her health" (1804), that Hobhouse included in a small volume he presented to his future wife.

It was left to Elizabeth Barrett, however, to write what would become, as we have seen, the most famous of the English poems on Strangford's formulation of what he took to be Camões's main themes and principal subjects. She would combine the details of the Portuguese poet's life as arranged and highlighted by Strangford with the refrain from Strangford's own rather free and clearly expanded translation of what he called one of Camões's "madrigals"—"and sweetest eyes that e'er were seen!"

That Strangford's poem, not strictly a translation, is really a poem on a Camonean theme becomes immediately apparent when we look at a more literal translation of Camões's own ten-line poem:

> My heart has been stolen;
> And love, seeing my anger,
> Has said: it was taken
> By the most beautiful eyes
> That I have ever seen.
> Supernatural charms
> Have it imprisoned.
> And if Love can reason,
> My Lady, by all the signs
> *You* have possessed my heart.[41]

It is of course Strangford's one-line rendering of Camões's fourth and fifth lines "And sweetest eyes that e'er were seen!" and his example in turning that line into a refrain that lie behind Elizabeth Browning's romantic poem "Catarina to Camoëns." But those facts do not tell the poem's whole story. The circumstances surrounding its composition are highly suggestive.

It has been known since 1969, with the publication of the nine-month diary Elizabeth Barrett kept at Hope's End from 4 June 1831 to 23 April 1832, just when the poem was written. On 16 November 1831 she entered in her diary: "a reading evening down stairs!—. . . over Camoens, & Moliére!—" The next day she returned to her diary to note: "reading Camoens last night, suggested what I have been writing this morning— 'Catarina to Camoens'. I do not dislike it." Whether or not she finished a version of the poem the day she started it is not known. It is known, however, that she felt a certain satisfaction about the composed poem by 30 November, for she was able, on that date, to enter in her diary laconically: "I began to write my Caterina in Annie's album."[42]

Why should Camões's star-crossed love for Catarina de Ataide have appealed to Elizabeth Barrett at this time? No answer can be entirely satisfactory, of course, but some conjecture is warranted. The oldest of Edward Barrett Moulton-Barrett's twelve children, Elizabeth was then twenty-five. After the death of her mother in 1828, her father had assumed the awesome burden of bringing up his children alone. There appeared to be no real prospects for marriage for the poet who spent much of her time convalescing from persistent illness, partly because of the isolation fostered by such illnesses but mainly because of her father's uniform opposition to marriage for any and all his children. Add to this two further facts: first, that she was deeply attached to her father, once saying that her "best hope" was "to die beneath his eyes"; and secondly, that during this period Elizabeth considered herself a deeply loyal protégé of Hugh Boyd, the blind scholar who, considerably her senior, supported, encouraged, and tutored her in her intellectual and poetic pursuits.[43] Pathetically sad is the story of her friendship with Boyd. "Great zeal, a fantastic memory, a narrow mind, an obstinate self-righteousness, a passion for esoteric detail and unimportant knowledge had made Mr. Boyd a pedant," write Browning's biographers.

Yet Boyd's "blindness, his ineffectuality, his loneliness, his eagerness for fellowship in study and learning had made him a pathetic and rather lovable pedant."[44] Older, and married, if rather indifferently so, Boyd was a safe friend for the young poet. But he was hardly a beau ideal. To give that fanciful gallant a name, she turned repeatedly to literature. How many other poets preceded Camões in Elizabeth's fancy and just who they were are questions not readily answered, but in November 1831 it was Strangford's Camões who had surfaced. For, as Strangford noted, "gallantry was the leading trait in the disposition of Camoens"; "woman was to him as a ministering angel, and for the little joy which he tasted in life, he was indebted to her."[45] Elizabeth might well have identified with Camões's Catarina, dying young, no longer even hoping at the last to see her exiled "lover-poet, romantic and pathetic."[46] Indeed, as Strangford explains, "'Love . . . inspired him [Camões] with the glorious resolution of conquering the obstacles which fortune had placed between him and felicity,' only to find, when his heroism had won him back his place at court, that Caterina had died in his absence."[47] Such was the myth around which Elizabeth wove her fantasy of the inspired, inspiring young lovely on her deathbed as she would address her absent, adoring poet-lover. She will even imagine the poet's late visit to her tomb, as she questions:

> *Will* you come? when I'm departed
>   Where all sweetnesses are hid—
> When thy voice, my tender-hearted,
>   Will not lift up either lid.
>   Cry, O lover,
>   Love is over!
> Cry beneath the cypress green—
> 'Sweetest eyes, were ever seen.'[48]

All the central themes of the twenty-five-year-old Elizabeth's secluded life are here: solitude, exile, devotion to poets (and poetry), unconsummated love, and early death. It is no wonder that Robert Browning, having fallen in love first with the lady's poetry and then with the lady herself, would choose to conduct his courtship of the lady through the substance of her poetry.

There is a postscript to this account of Elizabeth Barrett Browning's "Catarina to Camoëns." It will be recalled that Camões composed poetry both in Portuguese and Spanish, and, further, that he had actually written his famous poem extolling his lover's eyes in Spanish. Strangford then expanded on the original as he rendered it in English. Not a translator from the Portuguese, Elizabeth Barrett expanded on Camões in another way. Drawing on Strangford's version as well as on his prose account of Camões's life, she invented a chapter missing from the biographical accounts. It is only meet, then, that "Catarina to Camoëns" should itself make its way, sooner or later, into Portuguese. And it is especially appropriate that the task should have fallen to one of Portugal's two greatest poets, and Camões's twentieth-century successor. The modernist Fernando Pessoa— a poet to be ranked with T.S. Eliot, W.B. Yeats, Ezra Pound, Wallace Stevens, Paul Valéry, Antonio Machado, and Rilke— translated Mrs. Browning's poem at some point, it appears, during the second decade of the twentieth century. The translation, "Catarina a Camões," is faithful to the original, with one important exception: the poem's refrain. Instead of Mrs. Browning's "These poor eyes, you called, I ween, / Sweetest eyes, were ever seen!" Pessoa adopted a line from a different poem by Camões: "Who sees, my Lady, manifestly clear / The lovely being of your beautiful eyes."[49]

It was in Fernando Pessoa's distinguished translation that Catarina's deathbed musings achieved that Portuguese expression which Camões's original poem—the poem in Spanish that started the cycle just traced—had not. Thus it was that Strangford's conjectural reconstruction of the young Catarina de Ataide's poignant love for Camões as fleshed out by Elizabeth Barrett found a place in the literary history of Camões's own native land.

"Catarina to Camoëns" did its best work among the poets, from Robert Browning and Edgar Allan Poe to Herman Melville and Emily Dickinson—an unacknowledged scarlet thread in the strong nineteenth-century currents of romantic sentiment. It helped to determine form and substance in Edgar Allan Poe's most famous poem.

4

Poe's Knowledge

Elizabeth Barrett Browning's poetry was known and admired by two of America's greatest fiction writers of the first sixty years of the nineteenth century, Herman Melville and Edgar Allan Poe. Whereas Melville also knew Camões's work directly, it was through Poe's intense reading of Elizabeth Barrett Browning's poetry that he suffered his Camonean influence. Yet Poe also knew of Camões more directly, however, and that matter should be attended to before turning to what might be called his Camonean reading of Elizabeth Barrett Browning.

Under "Marginalia," in the *United States Magazine, and Democratic Review* in 1844, Poe included this item:

> Here is an edition [*Camöens*—Genoa—1798], which, so far as microscopical excellence and absolute accuracy of typography are concerned, might well be prefaced with the phrase of the Koran—"There is *no* error in this book." We cannot call a single inverted *o* an error—*can* we? But I am really as glad of having found that inverted *o*, as ever was a Columbus or an Archimedes. What, after all, are continents discovered, or silversmiths exposed? Give us a good *o* turned upside-down, and a whole herd of bibliomanic Arguses overlooking it for years.[1]

The first thing to note here is that no one has yet turned up evidence that there ever was any such edition as a *Camöens* published in Genoa in 1798. "Poe's 'Genoa, 1798' is a mystifying hoax, wrong in place and time," Burton Pollin has decided, for "no Genoese edition close to 1798 is listed for the great 1580 epic of Luis Vaz de Camoens (1524?-1580)."[2] Perhaps the reference to Columbus reminded him of the great sailor's (putative) natal city. But there is more. It is not evident that Poe had a first-hand knowledge of *Os Lusíadas* in any edition (original or translation), even though he returned to the topic of the near-perfect edition of Camões (identifying it accurately this time) in a paragraph under the rubric "Supplementary Pinakidia" in the *Southern Literary Messenger* (1848): "The magnificent edition of Camoen's As Lusiadas printed in 1817 by Dom Jose Souza, assisted by Didot, is perhaps the most immaculate specimen of typography in existence. In a few copies, however *one* error was discovered occasioned by one of the letters in the word Lusitano getting misplaced during the working of a sheet."[3]

In *Bibliographia Camoniana* (1880) the Portuguese scholar Theophilo Braga describes this edition: *"Os Lusiadas, Poema epico de Luiz de Camões,* a new, correct edition brought out by Dom José Maria de Sousa Botelho, Morgado de Matheus, member of the Academia Real das Sciencias de Lisboa. Paris, in the typography shop of Firmin Didot, Printer to the King and to the Institute. MDCCCXVII. 4° Atlantico."[4] He names all the collaborators—designers, engravers, artists—who worked on this "beautiful typographical monument consecrated to the glory of the *Lusíadas.*" Of the 210 copies, 182 were "presented to libraries and celebrated personages throughout Europe."[5]

Poe's knowledge of the "celebrated edition" by Souza Botelho seems to derive from Isaac Disraeli's essay on "Errata" in his *Curiosities of Literature,* a popular work of which there were several editions.

> Whether such a miracle as an immaculate edition of a classical author does exist, I have never learnt; but an attempt has been made to obtain this glorious singularity—and was as nearly realized as is perhaps possible; the magnificent edition of *As Luciadas* [*sic*] of Camoens, by Dom Joze Souza, in 1817. This amateur spared no prodigality of cost and labour, and flattered himself that by the assistance of Didet [*sic*], not a single typographical error should be found in that splendid volume. But an error was afterwards discovered in some of the copies, occasioned by one of the letters in the word *Lusitano* having got misplaced during the working of one of the sheets. It must be confessed that this was an *accident* or *misfortune*—rather than an *Erratum!*[6]

Pollin has enlisted the aid of the Library of Congress staff in an attempt to verify the alleged error in *Lusitano*, but in vain. Other errors have been found—*pdoer* instead of *poder* and *aprende* rather than *apprende*—but none involving *Lusitano*.

Pollin does not identify Disraeli's source but it seems highly likely that the story of the imperfection in the perfect edition of Camões's work can be traced to John Adamson's *Memoirs of the Life and Writings of Luis de Camoens*. Published in 1820, this work was well-known and readily available in Poe's and Disraeli's day. Of the 1817 edition done by Dom José Maria de Sousa-Botelho, a friend with whom he was in frequent contact, Adamson writes: "To make the edition also worthy of the poet, he had procured the assistance of M. Didot, hoping that by their joint attention, not a single typographical error should be found in the volume"; to which, he adds a footnote: "An error was afterwards discovered in some of the copies, caused by one of the letters in the word *Lusitano* having got misplaced during the working of one of the sheets. Dom Joze has had this leaf reprinted, and has sent copies of it to the several libraries wherein his work was deposited."[7] Had either Poe or Disraeli included the last sentence of Adamson's footnote, it would have become obvious to researchers at the Library of Congress checking for *Lusitano* misprints why they were unable to find any such thing.

Poe does not mention Adamson's work. But anyone acquainted with this two-volume work would know that Camões on several occasions—in the lyrics and in his epic—writes (eponymously) about a woman or (generically) women named Leonor.[8] In Adamson, Poe might have found the song in which Leonor laments the absence—perhaps the loss—of her lover, beginning:

> At the spring Leonor
> Washing her things, and weeping,
> And asking her friends:
> Have you seen my love?
> (Na fonte está Leonor,
> Lavando a talha, e chorando,
> A's amigas perguntando:
> Vistes lá o meu amor.)[9]

It does not seem far-fetched to suggest that Poe derived from Camões's various Leonors his own various Leonores—the "lost Lenore," whose absence is the catalyst for the speaker's self-revelation in "The Raven," or the titular heroine of the poem "Lenore" or (a variant) the heroine of the story "Eleanora." Yet it was such similitudes—especially striking to the Portuguese reader of Camões—that discouraged Poe's twentieth-century Portuguese translator, Fernando Pessoa, from using Poe's own name for his heroine. In fact, Pessoa chose not to "translate" the name of Poe's heroine at all. Rather than risking the inevitable cultural resonances, were he to employ the name Leonor, Pessoa chose to leave nameless the heroine of "The Raven." Poe's lines, "From my books surcease of sorrow—sorrow for the lost Lenore—/ For the rare and radiant maiden whom the angels name Lenore—/ Nameless *here* for evermore," Pessoa translates: "To forget the loved one (in vain!), today among the celestial hosts—/ That one whose name is known to the celestial hosts/ But herein nameless forever more" ("P'ra esquecer [em vão!] a amada, hoje entre hostes celestiaes—/ Essa cujo nome sabem as hostes celestiaes,/ Mas sem nome aqui jamais!").[10]

What did Poe know about Camões's life? From reading Elizabeth Barrett's poetry he learned the story of Camões's fateful and ultimately sorrow-laden love for Catarina Ataide. He knew the prevailing romantic story that Camões had been sent into exile from the court of Lisbon because he loved Catarina, and that while he was in the Far East, Catarina had died. Poe had not only read Elizabeth Barrett's poem on the subject— "Catarina to Camoëns," expressed entirely in the dying heroine's voice—but in reviewing her book, *A Drama of Exile: and other poems* in the *Broadway Journal* for 4 and 11 January 1845, he listed "Catarina to Camoëns" among those poems he found worthy of some praise.

Poe considers as well Miss Barrett's poem "A Vision of Poets," which includes lines mentioning Camões:

> And Camoens, with that look he had,
> Compelling India's Genius sad
> From the wave through the Lusiad,
> With murmurs of a purple ocean

Indrawn in vibrative emotion
Along the verse![11]

But although Poe quotes and discusses the lines referring to
Æschylus, Euripides, and Goethe, he does not bring up those
referring to Camões.

Far more worthy of Poe's critical attention, however, is the
third poem that mentions Camões, "Lady Geraldine's Courtship." From this poem he quotes several lines, including these:

> Eyes, he said, now throbbing through me! are ye eyes that
>   did undo me?
> *Shining eyes like antique jewels set in Parian statue-stone!*
> Underneath that calm white forehead are ye ever burning
>   torrid
> O'er the desolate sand desert of my heart and life undone?[12]

Although he finds the poem imitative of Tennyson's "Locksley
Hall," he defends it nevertheless against criticism leveled at it
in *Blackwood's Magazine*. Now it is the considered opinion of
Thomas Ollive Mabbott, the modern editor of Poe's poems, that
"unquestionably the cardinal source of the final stanzaic form
of Poe's poem ["The Raven"] was Elizabeth Barrett's 'Lady
Geraldine's Courtship' (1844)."[13] In demonstration he quotes the
same lines Poe had quoted, adding to them the four succeeding lines along with a fifth and later line:

> With a rushing stir, uncertain, in the air, the purple curtain
> Swelleth in and swelleth out around her motionless pale brows;
> While the gliding of the river sends a rippling noise forever
> Through the open casement whitened by the moonlight's slant
>   repose.
> .   .   .   .
> Ever, evermore the while in a slow silence she kept smiling . . . .[14]

In "Lady Geraldine's Courtship" Poe, who quotes the stanza that
refers to Camões's great Italian predecessor Petrarch (as an example of verse unrecognizable as metered verse when flattened
out to look like prose), also encountered, a few stanzas later,
the following lines:

> And this morning as I sat alone within the inner
>   chamber
> With the great saloon beyond it, lost in pleasant
>   thought serene,
> For I had been reading Camoëns, that poem you
>   remember,
> Which his lady's eyes are praised in as the sweetest
>   ever seen.[15]

Certainly it is not far-fetched to think of this narrator depicted in the act of reading Camões as gray eminence in "The Raven." It is small wonder that when *The Raven and Other Poems* was published on 19 November 1845, Poe dedicated it "TO THE NOBLEST OF HER SEX— / TO THE AUTHOR OF 'THE DRAMA OF EXILE'— / TO MISS ELIZABETH BARRETT BARRETT, / OF ENGLAND, / I DEDICATE THIS VOLUME, / WITH THE MOST ENTHUSIASTIC ADMIRATION/ AND WITH THE MOST SINCERE ESTEEM. / E. A. P."[16]

Available to Poe, as it was to Elizabeth Barrett Browning, was Strangford's *Poems, from the Portuguese of Luis de Camoens.* Poe does not mention Strangford, but it is unlikely that he could have missed *Poems, from the Portuguese*, which went through more than a dozen editions on both sides of the Atlantic—including printings in Philadelphia, Boston, and Baltimore—after its first appearance in 1803.

Strangford's highly romanticized account of Camões's life pays considerable attention to his love for Catarina de Ataide and the death of that beautiful young woman. One can imagine what Poe—who announced in "The Philosophy of Composition" (1846) that "the death, then, of a beautiful woman is, unquestionably, the most poetical topic in the world"—would have thought of Strangford's anticipation of his notion. "There can scarcely be conceived a more interesting theme for the visions of romance," announced Strangford, "than the death of this young and amiable being."[17] "The circumstances of her fate are peculiarly favourable to the exercise of conjecture," continues Strangford. "She loved, she was beloved, yet unfortunate in her attachment, she was torn from the world at the early age of twenty; and we cannot but adorn her grave with some of the wildest flowers, which fancy produces. But her lot was enviable, compared to that of her lover."[18] These sentiments would have struck a chord in the American poet, who also decided that "the lips best suited for such topic [the death of a beautiful woman] are those of a bereaved lover."[19] Intriguingly, while both "The Raven" and "Catarina to Camoëns" are first-person monologues by bereaved lovers, "Lady Geraldine's Courtship"—like "The Raven"—is almost entirely in the voice of a disappointed (if not grieving) male lover.[20]

Even Poe's protests in "The Philosophy of Composition" regarding the poetic use of the refrain in "The Raven"—his decision to use one, his determination to employ it in a new way, his discovery of the principle of various repetition—have their Elizabeth Barrett cast. In "Catarina to Camoëns" she employs a refrain that is varied in three of its nineteen stanzas.

Reading "The Raven" against Elizabeth Barrett's poet's knowledge of Camões's sentimental life—particularly as it is reflected in "Lady Geraldine's Courtship" and "Catarina to Camoëns"—is not critically fanciful. But there is a way in which "The Raven" informs my understanding (admittedly anachronistically) of Camões's work and life that is fanciful. At the beginning of his study of Camões, Adamson considers the etymology of the poet's family name, coming down on the side of an intriguing explanation:

[H]ad the poet himself not mentioned in his Redondilhas [Iberian folk lyrics] a certain bird, the extraordinary discrimination of which as to the fidelity of its mistress has been celebrated by other authors; the idea as to the name of Camoens being derived from its appellation, might have been disregarded as unworthy of notice. All that may be necessary to state is, that the bird named Camão, which never survived the infidelity of the wife of its Lord, has been supposed by some to have supplied a name to the ancestry of the poet. The passage referred to is—

Experimentou-se alguã hora
Da Ave que chamão Camão,
Que, se da Casa, onde mora,
Ve adultera, a Senhora,
Morre de pura paixão.[21]

One mid–nineteenth-century dictionary defines *camão* as "an aquatic bird, larger than a chicken, with a sharp beak and blue feathers" ("ave aquatica, maior que a gallinha, de bico agudo e penas azues").[22] Elsewhere *camão* is defined as "a kind of bird with long red legs and bill, that drinketh as if he bit the water."[23] The same dictionary identifies the *camão* as the Latin *porphyrio*.[24] So, too, does Adamson, who explains that "the more ancient name of this extraordinary bird appears to have been Porphyrio." This information links both the biographical Camões and his sixteenth-century lyrics to Poe's poem "The Haunted Palace" (first published in 1839 and later incorporated in "The Fall of the House of Usher": "Wanderers in that happy valley / Through two luminous windows saw / Spirits moving musically / To a lute's well-tunèd law; / Round about a throne, were sitting / (Porphyrogene!) / In state his glory well befitting, / The ruler of the realm was seen."[25]

The linking in Camões's biography of the bird *camão* with adultery finds consonance in Esther Rashkin's analysis of "The Haunted Palace" as corroboration for her larger discovery that the major theme of "The Fall of the House of Usher" is illegitimacy. "[I]t must mean that this 'porphyrogenite' was falsely born in purple," she writes, "that he was not the son of the king, and that those who descend hereafter from him ('A hideous throng rush out forever') are doomed to perpetuate his illegitimacy."[26] Coincidentally, Adamson's observations on the etymology of Camões's name also suggest a link to Poe's most famous poem "The Raven" (1845), by way perhaps of Robert Browning's 1836 poem "Porphyria's Lover," still another poem about the death—this time murder—of a beautiful young woman. In his own way, each poet—Camões (especially in Strangford's versions), Robert Browning, and Poe—focuses on webs woven by the vexed passions of death, loss, love, and betrayal.[27]

But there is one final piece in the puzzle of Poe's knowledge of Camões. There is the parallel between the figure that emerges at the very end of the *Narrative of Arthur Gordon Pym, of Nantucket* and the figure that appears in the fifth canto of *Os Lusíadas*.[28] It will be recalled that, as darkness encroaches, Pym and Peters attempt desperately to navigate dangerous southern waters. The narrator constructs a final entry, under 22 March, which concludes abruptly with these three short sentences: "And now we rushed into the embraces of the cataract, where a chasm threw itself open to receive us. But there arose in our pathway a shrouded human figure, very far larger in its proportions than any dweller among men. And the hue of the skin of the figure was of the perfect whiteness of the snow."[29]

If speculation as to the possible source for Poe's conception of this final, threatening and intimidating, more than human, white-skinned figure has not extended to Camões, it seems obvious to the reader of *Os Lusíadas* that Poe's source is the Portuguese epic.[30] This "shrouded human figure" derives from Adamastor, the Spirit of the Cape of Storms, who in Canto V of Camões's epic confronts the Portuguese sailors as they struggle mightily to round the Cape of the monster's "Antarctic world."[31]

> Não acabava, quando ũa figura
> Se nos mostra no ar, robusta e válida,
> De disforme e grandíssima estatura,
> O rosto caregado, a barba esquálida,
> Os olhos encovados, e a postura
> Medonha e má, e a cor terrena e pálida[.][32]

This description of Adamastor, "the brutal giant who frightens men by his revolting appearance,"[33] is rendered by Camões's two principal English translators of *Os Lusíadas* (prior to the nineteenth century) in images and language that anticipate Poe's description of his own dreaded figure. Richard Fanshawe's spirited version of 1655 reads:

> I had not ended, when a *humane* Feature
> Appear'd to us ith'*Ayre*, Robustious, ralli'd
> Of *Heterogeneal* parts, of *boundless* Stature,
> A *Clowd* in's *Face*, a *Beard* prolix and squallid:
> *Cave-Eyes*, a *gesture* that betray'd ill *nature*,
> And a worse mood, a clay *complexion* pallid[.][34]

But closer in details to Poe's description in *Pym* is William Julius Mickle's 1776 version:

> Appall'd we saw an hideous Phantom glare;
> High and enormous o'er the flood he tower'd,
> And thwart our way with sullen aspect lour'd:
> An earthy paleness o'er his cheeks was spread,
> Erect uprose his hairs of wither'd red;
> Writhing to speak his sable lips disclose,
> Sharp and disjoin't his gnashing teeth's blue rows;
> His haggard beard flow'd quivering on the wind[.][35]

Between Fanshawe's 1655 translation and Mickle's 1776 translation Voltaire had commented on the Adamastor passage. In 1729, in his "An Essay on Epick Poetry" (first published in English in London), Voltaire writes: "When the Fleet is sailing in the Sight of the *Cape of Good-Hope*, call'd then the *Cape of the Storms*, a formidable Shape appears to them, walking in the Depth of the Sea; his Head reaches to the Clouds, the Storms, the Winds, the Thunders, and the Lightnings hang about him; his Arms are extended over the Waves. 'Tis the Guardian of that foreign Ocean unplough'd before by any Ship."[36]

Mickle, adducing "Voltaire, and the foreign Critics," affirms "that the fiction of the apparition of the Cape of Tempests, in sublimity and awful grandeur of imagination, stands unsurpassed in human composition."[37] In words that apply as well to the shrouded figure in *Pym*, C.M. Bowra writes of Adamastor: "the grisly and revolting phantom is an apt symbol of the horrors which may well appal those who break into waters where no men have sailed before."[38] This link between *Pym* and *Os Lusíadas* suggests that Poe's knowledge of Camões was greater than anyone has suspected, extending, perhaps, to the way Poe, writing before *Moby-Dick*, handles seascapes and storms in this, his longest narrative.

5

Melville's Figural Artist

Of Herman Melville's interest in the life and works of Luis de Camões there exists ample evidence. First, there continues to sing out from the pages of his novel *White-Jacket* (1850) the cries of the "matchless and unmatchable Jack Chase," who appears to have been the young sailor Melville's beau ideal: "For the last time, hear Camoens, boys!"[1] Secondly, from the pages of Melville's encyclopedic novel *Moby-Dick* (1851) come unmistakable references to Camões's poem of empire *Os Lusiádas* (1572), "the great epic of the ocean."[2] Third, among the books in Melville's library (including books owned by Melville or known to have been read by him) we can with confidence number *The Lusiad: or The Discovery of India*, translated by William Julius Mickle (1776); *Poems, from the Portuguese of Luis de Camoens*, translated by Lord Viscount Strangford (1803); and *Poems of Elizabeth Barrett Browning* (1854), the last of which includes Miss Barrett's "Catarina to Camoëns," a poem well known to Melville and useful to him, it has been proposed, in the writing of his ambitious long poem *Clarel* (1876).[3] Fourth, several of Melville's poems allude to or draw upon Camões's work. And, finally, as culminating evidence of his abiding interest in the Portuguese poet, Melville has left us "Camoëns," a poem made up of paired sonnets entitled "Camoëns" and "Camoëns in the Hospital."

Yet, important as Camões was to Melville, it was not until 1924 that their names were first linked in a scholarly piece. Without insisting on influence, Merritt Y. Hughes made the connection in an essay commemorating the four hundredth anniversary of Camões's birth by relating the white whale Moby Dick to the giant Adamastor.[4] It would be another five years before a second critic, Lewis Mumford, would again bring up the matter.[5] That Mumford was deliberately following up on Hughes's hint, moreover, is highly possible. The same issue of the *New York Evening Post Literary Review* carrying Hughes's essay also carried one of Mumford's book reviews.

Hughes's and Mumford's modest references to the links between Melville and Camões stand out nearly alone in Melville scholarship until Newton Arvin's seminal pages on the subject of Camões and Melville appeared in his American Men of Letters volume on Melville in 1950. "It is hard indeed not to feel that *Moby Dick* would have been somewhat different from what it is," decided Arvin, "if Melville had not known the *Lusiads*."[6] Arvin's work was followed by Leon Howard's consideration in his biography of 1951,[7] a work drawing upon the documentary materials assembled by Jay Leyda for his two volumes of *The Melville Log* published in the same year,[8] and by Lawrance Thompson's provocative study *Melville's Quarrel With God* (1952). Incidentally, Thompson became the first critic to attend in detail to the two soliloquies constituting Melville's poem "Camoëns."[9] In the same year, 1952, appeared the Hendricks House edition of *Moby-Dick*, edited with copious explanatory notes (in which references to and echoes of *The Lusiads* were identified) by Luther S. Mansfield and Howard P. Vincent.[10]

The 1960s brought the first recognition of the Camões-Melville connection from scholars in the Portuguese-speaking countries of Brazil and Portugal. First there was a passing reference by the Brazilian Augusto Meyer,[11] and then, in *The Portuguese and the Tropics* (called in the original *O Luso e o Trópico*), a second Brazilian, Gilberto Freyre, incorporated considerations of both writers into his elaboration of his immediately appealing if somewhat controversial theory of luso-tropicalism.[12] The publication of Freyre's influential book prompted some appropriate remarks on the subject of Camões and Melville by the Portuguese scholar Américo da Costa Ramalho.[13]

These pioneering efforts paved the way for most of the subsequent studies of the Camões-Melville connection. Salient among these are Brian F. Head's piece published in English in Brazil in 1964,[14] William H. Shurr's contextual commentary on Melville's poems in 1972,[15] Edwin Haviland Miller's suggestive pages in 1975,[16] my own article in 1978 on Melville's re-reading in 1867 of Lord Strangford's *Poems, from the Portuguese* (an expanded version of which appeared in 1982),[17] Lucy M. Freibert's study (already mentioned).[18] Further studies of the Camões-Melville connection include Alexandrino E. Severino's 1987 essay on Camonean echoes and traces in *Moby-Dick*, a piece based on his talk at the Modern Language Association meetings in New York in 1972,[19] and John P. McWilliams's brief but acute commentary in his 1989 study, *The American Epic*,[20] on Melville's reliance upon William Julius Mickle's eighteenth-century translation of Camões's verse epic for his own prose transformation of the form of the epic, *Moby-Dick*. He, too, like Merritt Hughes in 1924 and Alexandrino Severino in 1972, associates Adamastor, the Spirit of the Cape, with Moby Dick, the white whale that Captain Ahab's obsession turns into the agent of destructive doom for the ship's whole complement—officers and crew, save only Ishmael, who alone is saved to tell us the story.

Yet for all of this, there is still much to be done, for the subject of Camões and Melville—their personal and intertextual relationships—is far from exhausted. The following are two or three ideas that cannot be pursued here: Mickle distinguishes between John Milton's *Paradise Lost* and Camões's *The Lusiads*: "In contradistinction to the Iliad and Æneid, the Paradise Lost has been called the Epic Poem of Religion. In the same manner may the Lusiad be named the Epic Poem of Commerce."[21] Is it far-fetched to suggest that Melville in *Moby-Dick*, taking hints from all earlier epics, but specifically the notion suggested by Mickle, attempted, by focusing on whaling, to write the great American Epic Poem of Commerce, a point touched on by McWilliams? Moreover, just as Camões wrote his celebratory poem in the years of Portugal's decline as a nation of explorers, so, too, did Melville choose to romanticize the industry of whaling when it had fallen into decline and disrepute.[22] Ishmael puts the matter succinctly in "The Advocate" (chapter 24). "This business of whaling has somehow come to be regarded among landsmen as a rather unpoetical and disreputable pursuit," he explains. "Therefore, I am all anxiety to convince ye, ye landsmen, of the injustice hereby done to us hunters of whales."[23] And as for Ishmael, was not Melville's decision to make his first-person narrator a member of Captain Ahab's crew anticipated by Camões's decision to place himself, both ahistorically and anachronistically, on Vasco da Gama's ship of exploration? These and other matters—largely in the case of *Moby-Dick* (say, the shared monitions and prophecies before the initial sailings[24]), but also in Melville's last work of fiction, *Billy Budd*—are still invitingly open to scholarly and critical investigation.

But what I shall do here is something else. I shall look at the ways in which Camões's life and work served Herman Melville the poet, both in his life and his poetry. In short, I shall examine the evidence supporting the notion that not only is Camões present in some of Melville's poems, but that the circumstances of Camões's life became increasingly emblematic to Melville himself in the last decade of his life, a period almost exclusively devoted to poetry.

To begin with, there is a poem from Melville's first collection of poetry, published in 1866, a year after the end of the Civil War. In *Battle-Pieces and Aspects of War* appears the poem entitled "The Fortitude of the North, under the Disaster of the Second Manassas":

> No shame they take for dark defeat
>   While prizing yet each victory won,
> Who fight for the Right through all retreat,
>   Nor pause until their work is done.
> The Cape-of-Storms is proof to every throe;
>   Vainly against that foreland beat
> Wild winds aloft and wilder waves below:
> The black cliffs gleam through rents in sleet
> When the livid Antarctic storm-clouds glow.[25]

The poem turns on a simple comparison. The Northern army, defeated for the second time at Manassas, is compared to the Cape-of-Storms, that foreland whose "black cliffs" are impervious to winds and waves, to sleet and storm-clouds.

This rather direct poem has not been materially misread. Yet that it is touched by Camões has gone undetected. Indeed Melville's reference to "The Cape-of-Storms" recalls Camões's "Cabo Tormentorio" (V, 50, 65; X, 37), which Mickle renders as "the Cape of Tempests."[26] Robert Penn Warren and Hennig

Cohen, two of Melville's most perceptive readers, too readily identify "Cape-of-Storms" as a reference to Cape Horn. "For Melville, Cape Horn, the 'Cape-of-Storms,' was a place of great tribulation," writes Cohen. "He had rounded it as a seaman and a passenger, and in his journal on August 7, 1860, gave it this telling description: 'Horrible snowy mountains—black, thunder-cloud woods—gorges—hell-landscapes.'"[27] Warren, on the other hand, linking "The Fortitude of the North, under the Disaster of the Second Manassas" with an earlier poem, "The March Into Virginia, Ending in the First Manassas," draws on the reference to "The Cape-of-Storms" and the appearance of the term "throe" in both poems to insist: "Once the nature of the self and the terms of life are clear, one can bear the 'throe.' So here the theme of the poem goes back to Melville's old obsessive theme. First Manassas is like the Horn that must be rounded if man is to be fully man."[28] But it is not Cape Horn that is traditionally known as the Cape of Storms. The key, of course, is not in Melville's references to Cape Horn in a letter or an entry in his journal,[29] but in his novels. In "The Spirit-Spout," chapter 51 of *Moby-Dick*, Ishmael cries out: "Cape of Good Hope, do they call ye? Rather Cape Tormentoto, as called of yore."[30] And earlier, in *White-Jacket*, Melville writes: "Turned on her heel by a fierce West Wind, many an outward-bound ship has been driven across the Southern Ocean to the Cape of Good Hope—*that* way to seek a passage to the Pacific. And that stormy Cape, I doubt not, has sent many a fine craft to the bottom, and told no tales."[31]

When we turn to *John Marr and Other Sailors with Some Sea-Pieces*, Melville's second collection of lyric poems published in 1888, we find Camões all but named in "Crossing the Tropics," a twenty-one line poem divided into three stanzas of five lines each followed by a couplet. This is a nicely turned love poem that would not usually call for special attention. Given the topic of Camões's presence in Melville's poetry, however, I would point to the reference to Vasco da Gama in lines ten and twelve:

> By day the blue and silver sea
> And chime of waters blandly fanned—

> Nor these, nor Gama's stars to me
> May yield delight, since still for thee
> I long as Gama longed for land.[32]

Since Mickle's translation of *The Lusiads* was most likely Melville's principal text for knowledge of Vasco da Gama, it would appear reasonable to look in that place for a possible source for Melville's references in this poem. Brian Head points to such a place, Canto 5, stanzas 13-15, which contain these lines:[33]

> Before us now another Pole Star glows . . .
> Full to the south a shining cross appears[.][34]

Melville echoes these lines at the very opening of his poem:

> While now the Pole Star sinks from sight
> The Southern Cross it climbs the sky[.][35]

Melville's use of Camões in "Crossing the Tropics" is not particularly suggestive. His borrowings from *The Lusiads* are tributary, of course, but only in the way a professional might tip his hat at the achievement of a fellow craftsman. The borrowings in this poem are not deeply personal, as they will become in other poems.

One other poem in this collection deserves a new look. Head has suggested that "The Enviable Isles" may have been "at least partly inspired by Camoëns' 'Isle of Love.'"[36]

> Through storms you reach them and from storms are free.
>   Afar descried, the foremost drear in hue,
> But, nearer, green; and, on the marge, the sea
>   Makes thunder low and mist of rainbowed dew.
>   But, inland, where the sleep that folds the hills
> A dreamier sleep, the trance of God, instills—
>   On uplands hazed, in wandering airs aswoon,
> Slow-swaying palms salute love's cypress tree
>   Adown in vale where pebbly runlets croon
> A song to lull all sorrow and all glee.
> Sweet-fern and moss in many a glade are here,

> Where, strown in flocks, what cheek-flushed myriads lie
> Dimpling in dream—unconscious slumberers mere,
> While billows endless round the beaches die.[37]

Head adduces passages from Mickle's translation of Camões's description of this place (Canto 9), which I shall not reproduce here. The Melville who had visited the, at least superficially, Edenic islands of the Pacific and who would incorporate those experiences in his early books, *Typee* and *Mardi*, did not miss, one can be sure, as Head first pointed out, Camões's verses on the Blessed Isles as the locus of seductive beauty and enticing serenity. The suggestion that Melville's poem is indebted to Camões is plausible, though there is some likelihood that the similarities point as well to a more generic debt the two of them share with Homer, Virgil, Milton, Dante, Spenser, Ariosto, and Tasso.[38]

Head's additional suggestion that the four-line poem "In a Garret," published in *Timoleon, Etc.* in 1891, can be related to the life of Camões has not hitherto been picked up by Melville scholars. It has considerable merit, though the case Head makes for it can be enhanced. "In a Garret" reads:

> Gems and jewels let them heap—
> Wax sumptuous as the Sophi:
> For me, to grapple from Art's deep
> One dripping trophy![39]

Head points to the fact that in *White-Jacket* Melville has Jack Chase, that great admirer of Camões's poetry, refer to "the cave at the end of the flowery, winding way, where Camoëns, according to tradition, composed certain parts of his Lusiad." He then employs an original meaning for "garret"—that is, "shelter"—and equates "shelter" with "cave" to make his link in this poem between Melville and Camões. One additional connection that he does not make is the one implicit in the phonological similitudes in the words "garret" and "grotto," the latter a term used to describe the place in Macao made available to Camões while he was exiled from Goa and where he worked on his epic poem. As John Adamson writes, "A Grotto is shewn at Macáo, wherein tradition reports Camoëns spent great part of the time, during which he was employed on the completion of his poem: accounts of it may be seen in the works of the authors, who have recorded the proceedings of the two last embassies sent from England to China. It is still called The Grotto of Camoëns."[40] Adamson includes an illustration of the Grotto, a woodcut drawn from a sketch of this retreat in Sir William Ouseley's *Oriental Collections*. The same information was available to Melville in Henry Wadsworth Longfellow's massive anthology of European poetry in translation first published in 1845, where he could have read that in Macao Camoës "spent much of his time in a grotto overlooking the sea, and there the greater part of the 'Lusiad' is said to have been written. The place is still shown to strangers as the Grotto of Camoens."[41] In *White-Jacket* (1850) Melville himself has Jack Chase announce: "Yes, I've sailed over the very track that Camoens sailed—round the East Cape into the Indian Ocean. I've been in Don Jose's garden, too, in Macao, and bathed my feet in the blessed dew of the walks where Camoens wandered before me. Yes, White-Jacket, and I have seen and sat in the cave at the end of the flowery, winding way, where Camoens, according to tradition, composed certain parts of his Lusiad. Ay, Camoens was a sailor once!"[42]

In 1964, the same year in which Head published his speculative reading of the poem, appeared Hennig Cohen's *Selected Poems of Herman Melville*, a carefully prepared edition armed with commentary. What he says about "In a Garret" has some bearing on the question of how Camões functions as a presence in the poem. Cohen begins by glossing Melville's reference in the second line of the poem to "Sophi."[43] He sees it as referring to St. Sophia in Constantinople, which Melville visited in 1856 while on his travels in the Near East. "'Supurb [*sic*] interior,'" wrote Melville in his journal, "'Precious marbles Porphyry & Verd antique. Immense magnitude of the building.'" In a second entry, also quoted by Cohen, he added: "'Owing to its peculair [*sic*] form St: Sophia viewed near to, looks as partly underground; as if you saw but the superstructure of some immense temple, yet to be disinterred. You step *down* to enter.'"[44] Fortified by Melville's references, Cohen interprets the poem as follows:

The impression of the sumptuousness of the building is retained in the poem and the need to descend in order to enter it may lie behind the nautical imagery of grappling for objects from the depths of the sea. However, the word "grapple" also indicates the strain and conflict involved in plumbing the depths. Melville rejects great riches accumulated through the efforts of others for the opportunity to grapple for a single gem himself. If he had in mind the significance of the name St. Sophia, in English "Holy Wisdom," then the poem hints at an opposition between philosophy and art in the process of artistic creativity.[45]

"Sophi" refers, of course, first of all to the Persian princes whose waxing sumptuously results from an accumulation of gems and jewels. (Whether or not "Sophi" also refers to "the Magian priests" who brought myrrh and frankincense—in Melville's poem symbolized by "wax"—as William Bysshe Stein has suggested, I shall not venture.)[46] But it is Melville's nautical imagery, unexamined as such by Head or Stein but pointed to by Cohen, that enhances the likelihood that Camões is present in the poem, however buried and disguised. Within Melville's asserted choice—"For me to grapple from Art's deep / One dripping trophy"—are references to two poets: Schiller and Camões. Cohen points to Schiller and his poem "The Diver":

> Titles which Melville considered but discarded include "Ambition," "Schiller's Ambition," and "The Spirit of Schiller." His copy of Schiller's *Poems and Ballads* in the translation of Edward Bulwer Lytton shows marked passages in "The Diver." This ballad is about a brave, ambitious squire who plunges into a maelstrom to recover a golden cup in response to the challenge of the king. When he succeeds, the king offers him the hand of his daughter if he dives for the goblet a second time. The squire does so and is drowned though he himself had warned that one should not "stretch too far the wide mercy of Heaven." "In a Garret" shares the idea of the risks involved in plunging for "One dripping trophy."[47]

Without gainsaying the strong evidence that Schiller was on Melville's mind when he entitled his poem on art and creativity, I would argue that at least subconsciously Camões was also on his mind. In Mickle's pages on Camões's life Melville had learned of the legendary survival of Camões's manuscript of *The Lusiads*. "[D]esirous to return to Goa," Mickle tells us, "he set sail, but was shipwrecked in the gulph near the mouth of the river Mehon on the coast of China. All he had acquired was lost in the waves: his poems, which he held in one hand, while he swimmed with the other, were all he found himself possessed of, when he stood friendless on the unknown shore."[48] In Book 7 of *The Lusiads* Camões refers to the shipwreck:

> Now blest with all the wealth fond hope could crave,
> Soon I beheld that wealth beneath the wave
> For ever lost; myself escaped alone,
> On the wild shore all friendless, hopeless, thrown;
> My life, like Judah's heaven-doom'd king of yore,
> By miracle prolong'd; yet not the more
> To end my sorrows: woes succeeding woes
> Belied my earnest hopes of sweet repose:
> In place of bays around my brows to shed
> Their sacred honours, o'er my destined head
> Foul Calumny proclaim'd the fraudful tale,
> And left me mourning in a dreary jail.[49]

Obviously, one can point to the choice made by the shipwrecked Camões—his manuscript over any other kind of wealth—as not unrelated to the choice of "one dripping trophy" from "Art's deep" indicated in Melville's poem. To have grappled to keep *The Lusiads* from falling back into the depths of the subconscious ("Art" in Melville's poem) only to lose the manuscript itself to the very sea that is both emblematic and natural would have been the poet's greatest tragedy. *The Lusiads*, so saved from a form of what Joseph Conrad called the destructive element, stands as the kind of "dripping trophy" that Melville would prize over all of the Sophi's gems and jewels. As one of Melville's contemporaries put it in 1848, "With but a single plank to which he could cling for succor, he suffered all else to perish—the savings of his exile—all his earthly possessions save the treasure of his heart, and to rescue this he struggled with the mighty ocean and was victor! He rescued his poem and himself, not without difficulty, from a watery grave."[50] It occurs to me, more-

over, as I look back at Camões's lines just quoted, that in em-
ploying the phrase "myself escaped alone"—with its echo of
Job—Mickle anticipates Melville's use of the same Jobean verse
in *Moby-Dick* when, in the epilogue, Ishmael says: "And I only
am escaped alone to tell thee."[51]

Immediately preceding "In a Garret" in Cohen's edition of
Melville's poems appears the poem "The Garden of Metrodorus,"
also from the volume *Timoleon*:

> The Athenians mark the moss-grown gate
> And hedge untrimmed that hides the haven green:
> And who keeps here his quiet state?
> And shares he sad or happy fate
> Where never foot-path to the gate is seen?
> Here none come forth, here none go in,
> Here silence strange, and dumb seclusion dwell:
> Content from loneness who may win?
> And is this stillness peace or sin
> Which noteless thus apart can keep its dell?[52]

Cohen's commentary is pertinent to our investigation into the
matter of Camões's presence in Melville's poetry. He is alone,
among Melville's critics, in hinting at a connection, or at least
evidence of an affinity, between the sentiments expressed in
"The Garden of Metrodorus" and similar sentiments expressed
in Camões's poetry. Darrell Abel writes: "'The Garden of
Metrodorus'. . . symbolizes the cryptic character of the philosopher and his domain as seen by ordinary men, who may casu-
ally wonder about his esoteric experience but have no
conception of its realities."[53] Cohen, on the other hand, sees it
more as a poem about withdrawal and, perhaps by implica-
tion, estrangement: "Melville suggests that the withdrawal into
the silent, unkempt garden is in itself a puzzling response and
raises more questions than it answers: for example, questions
of whether the state of quietude is one of happiness or sadness,
peace or sin. But he himself was sympathetic to withdrawal."[54]
Cohen then follows up with this interesting sentence:

In his copy of Camoëns' poetry he marked this passage from
"Sonnet VI":

My senses lost, misjudging men declare
And Reason banish'd from her mental throne,
Because I shun the crowd, and dwell alone.[55]

These opening lines, marked by Melville in the copy of Strangford's *Poems, from the Portuguese* he acquired on 17 May 1867, were not the only lines so marked by the sympathizing author. In fact, the page appears as follows:

SONNET VI. (*V.N.*)

"Julgame a gente toda por perdido
Vendome tão entregue a meu cuydado," &c.

My senses lost, misjudging men declare,
  And Reason banish'd from her mental throne,
  Because I shun the crowd, and dwell alone
In the calm trance of undisturb'd despair,
Tears all my pleasure—all my comfort care!
  But I have known, from long experience known
  How vain the worship to those idols shown,
Which charm the world, and reign unrivall'd there:
Proud dreams of pow'r, and fortune's gilded glare,
  The lights that blaze in tall Ambition's tow'r,
  For such, let others waste life's little hour
In toil and weary search—but be it mine,
  Lady! to muse of thee—and in my bow'r
Pour to thy praise the soul-impassion'd line![56]

Here, too, as in "The Garden of Metrodorus," "the single-minded good man is crushed by less naive forces and cast out."[57] Here, with this poem by Camões, we can build a bridge between the Melville of "In a Garret," committed to Art and grappling for "one dripping trophy," and the Melville who, late in life, devoted one two-part poem to Camões.

    Among the some forty poems Melville left in manuscript at the time of his death in 1891 at the age of seventy-two—including poems on Shakespeare's Falstaff, Don Quixote, Montaigne—was, preeminently, a poem devoted to Camões. This poem remained unpublished until 1924, when it appeared under the rubric of "Miscellaneous Poems" in volume sixteen—*Poems*—of *The Works of Herman Melville* brought out by Constable, the British publisher. The poem has been reprinted several times since, of course, but never to my knowledge exactly as it first appeared in the Constable edition. It is the version published in Howard P. Vincent's Hendricks House edition of the *Collected Poems*, published in 1947, that has become standard. Yet since the Constable and Hendricks House versions both have authority in the extant manuscripts—the textual differences resulting from editorial decisions—it seems consonant with my present purpose to consider the longer, Constable version of the poem "Camoëns." Three minor typographical errors have been corrected silently.

CAMOENS
(*Before*)
And ever must I fan this fire?
Thus ever in flame on flame aspire?
Ever restless, restless, craving rest—
The Imperfect toward Perfection pressed!
Yea, for the God demands thy best.
The world with endless beauty teems,
And thought evokes new worlds of dreams:
Hunt then the flying herds of themes!
And fan, still fan, thy fervid fire,
Until thy crucibled gold shall show
That fire can purge as well as glow.
In ordered ardour, nobly strong,
Flame to the height of epic song.
(*After*)
CAMOENS IN THE HOSPITAL
What now avails the pageant verse,
Trophies and arms with music borne?
Base is the world; and some rehearse
How noblest meet ignoble scorn,
Vain now thy ardour, vain thy fire,
Delirium mere, unsound desire;
Fate's knife hath ripped thy chorded lyre.
Exhausted by the exacting lay,
Thou dost but fall a surer prey
To wile and guile ill understood;
While they who work them, fair in face,
Still keep their strength in prudent place,
And claim they worthier run life's race,
Serving high God with useful good.[58]

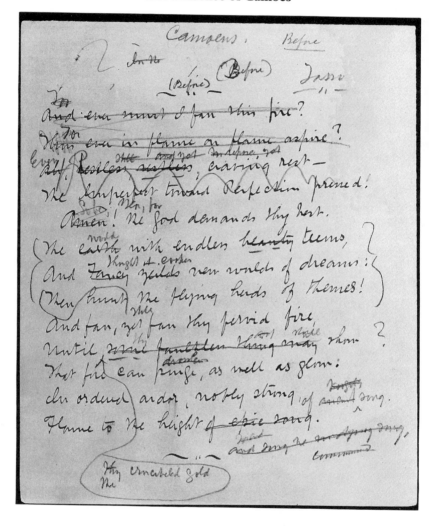

Manuscript of Herman Melville's *"Camoens (Before)."*

Much can be said about these two sonnets (and sonnets they are, though the first one, running to thirteen lines, can be called a sonnet manqué), but I shall limit myself to two or three observations. First, it will be immediately noted that in these first-person verses spoken in the voice of the Portuguese poet we

Manuscript of Melville's *"Camoens (After)."*

are intended to hear, in sequence, the voice, first, of the poet in mid-career and, secondly, the voice of the aging and infirm poet. In the former, the poet resorts to imagery of fire and crucibles to describe the poetic fervor he feels as he composes his epic song. In full stride, in the finest line in poem, he "hunt[s] then the flying herds of themes." Here, then, are his two metaphors: those of the poet at his forging, and the poet as hunter. The

speaker exudes strength, passion, and purpose. In the latter sonnet, subtitled, it will be recalled, "Camoëns in the Hospital,"
the tone is plaintive and recriminatory. "Vain now thy ardour,
vain thy fire," the poet laments. He has fallen victim, finally, to
his art. He has been "exhausted by the exacting lay" and is prey,
thus, to the "wiles" and "snares" (alternative reading in the
manuscript) of those who have been more prudent, those who
claim to have served "high God" in "practical mood" (again an
alternative manuscript reading). In this poem Melville once
again sounds the note, since heard in Ecclesiastes and acknowledged in *Moby-Dick*, of "the fine hammered steel of woe."[59]

There is, of course, ample justification in the accounts of
Camões known to Melville—those of his translators, Mickle and
Strangford—for the double portrait (before and after) Melville
gives us. Consider, for instance, the testimony of Josepe Indio,
who testified that he had been present in 1579 at the poet's death
in an alms-house: "What a lamentable thing to see so great a
genius so ill rewarded! I saw him die in an hospital in Lisbon,
without having a sheet (shroud) to cover him, after having tri-
umphed in the East Indies, and sailed 5500 leagues! What good
advice for those, who weary themselves night and day in study
without profit, as the spider weaves its webs to catch flies."[60]

It is of little matter that historians have questioned the historicity of such accounts, for the legend of the poet maligned
and neglected has a long history. Yet there is a puzzling fact
about the extant manuscript for this poem. The word "Tasso"
is written beside the rubrics of both verses of the poem. The
first sheet reads:

Camoëns *Before*
(Before)
~~In the~~ *Tasso*
(Before)

And the second one contains an explanatory tag:

Suggested by ~~his~~ a ~~p~~ bust of that poet
Tasso[.][61]

Melville of course knew both the poetry of Torquato Tasso and
the story of his woeful life. Available to him was the scholarship of Richard Henry Wilde, the poet and translator of Camões,

who entitled his book *Conjectures and Researches Concerning the Love, Madness & Imprisonment of Torquato Tasso*, published in New York in 1842. He knew as well Baroness de Staël-Holstein's *Germany*, in the second volume of which he scored and checked this passage: "The morbid sensibility of Tasso is well known, as well as the polished rudeness of his protector Alphonso, who, professing the highest admiration for his writings, shut him up in a mad-house, as if that genius which springs from the soul were to be treated like the production of a mechanical talent, by valuing the work while we despise the workman."[62] In 1857, in Europe on his way to the Levant, Melville made an obligatory visit to "St. Onofrio, church & monastery, where Tasso expired." "Tasso's prison," he wrote, "Mere cidercellar. Grated window, but not strong."[63]

In short, it is obvious that Tasso and Camões, melding somewhat in Melville's mind, became emblematic for him of the fate of the poet in societies in which there was, to borrow Strangford's words, a "decline of public spirit in matters of taste"—a "certain indication of political decay."[64] In 1881 Melville could have read in Richard Burton's *Camoens: His Life and His Lusiads*: "As Tasso, leaving the Hospital and Madhouse of St. Anne, found a last refuge in the Monastery of Sant 'Onofrio, so his *colto e buon Luigi* passed his latter days with the Religious of S. Domingos. Perhaps these were the only men, save the Licentiate Corrêa and a knot of personal friends, who could understand him."[65]

The fact of the matter is that in his last years, perhaps for a decade or more, Melville took to seeing analogs for his own fate in the histories of other literary figures, both fictional and historical. In this sense, Camões's fate was Tasso's fate, and their fate was Melville's own. As such, "Camoëns" is a poem about the seemingly universal experience of these national poets. It is as if the epic poet who had sung of Gama and Adamastor, the epic poet who had written of the First Crusade, and the epic novelist who had sung the tragedy of Ahab and Moby Dick, belong, ahistorically, to a cohort of genius, each member of which has been accused of madness. Yet, what each has done through his poetry, regardless of the low estate to which he has fallen in an infirm old age, remains his monument. This is the message proclaimed by Tasso, precociously for himself, in his sonnet on Camões, as translated by Mickle, which it will be recalled, comparing the poet to Vasco da Gama, concludes:

> Great as thou art, and peerless in renown,
> Yet thou to Camoens ow'st thy noblest fame;
> Farther than thou didst sail, his deathless song
> Shall bear the dazzling splendour of thy name;
> And under many a sky thy actions crown,
> While Time and Fame together glide along.[66]

Melville surely knew Tasso's poem, for it appears in Mickle's introduction to his English version of *The Lusiads*. For the Melville whose literary reputation had greatly declined in his last decades (though the demand for some of his fiction had never entirely disappeared), it must have seemed bootless to believe that his songs would prove to be "deathless," least of all the lay of *Moby-Dick*. Melville chose, then, in imagining the words of Camões (or Tasso) both in mid-career and at the end of his life, to bring out, first, the impassioned confidence and, then, the bitter disappointment attendant to a poet who fears that his work has come to nothing. Happily what might have seemed to be outrageously hubristic in Melville's later years— identifying himself with Camões and Tasso—has turned out, a century later, to be fairly close to the mark. *The Lusiads*, *Jerusalem Delivered*, *Moby-Dick*—merely to rehearse their titles suffices to make the point.[67]

In his study of the Camões-Melville relationship, Norwood Andrews, Jr. confirms that Camões was even more important to Melville than the echoes of, and references to, Camões's work that scholars have so far discovered would seem at first glance to indicate. Andrews calls attention to the fact that over his long career as a writer Melville found first uses and then re-uses for Camões.[68]

Those large implications in Melville's late use of Camões impose exigencies and responsibilities for the serious student of Melville and his work. What is the Melvillean to make of the fact that Melville insisted on superimposing his Camões on his Tasso? It is tenable to think that Melville identified closely with the Camões whose voice is dramatized in the two sonnets that constitute a single monologic poem. (He had already unmistakably registered such an identification in 1867 when he annotated tellingly his recently acquired copy of Strangford's translations of Camões's lyric poetry in ways that reflected his own wife's estrangement from him.) If this is so, what must the biographer make of the fact that in this late period of relative quietude (and reconciliation with the idea of living out his life with his wife and in marriage) Melville was still writing poems that are bitter in the words he gives us as spoken by his great predecessors, poems leveling charges of social neglect and personal abuse? Through these poems we can discover that Melville's conception of those predecessors as maligned, neglected writers of genius enabled him to link his fate with that of other unquestionably great writers who suffered grievously at the end of their lives. Melville, with his large measure of unrequited self-esteem, plugs himself into an archetype or paradigm (one that belongs as much to history as to literature) that tells us much about Melville's way of thinking about himself, at least at the time he was writing about Camões.

That Melville changed his mind not only about the title of the poem but about the identity of the poem's speaker suffices to tip us off that Melville at the end still saw himself—in "colossal cipher" (Ralph Waldo Emerson's words for Dante's audacity)—as a member of the pantheon of the great epic writers who in their own time have not been decently treated or adequately appreciated. And more. Was not Melville also implying that under the guise of history the author of *Moby-Dick* would some day come into his own? What, then, are the implications of all this for the biography of a writer who at the end of his life, in a tale about mutiny, turned to the themes of law and society, innocence and depravity, will and determinism? How, too, will the biographer measure the mind and personality of the Melville who would apply metaphorically to himself what was literally true for Tasso (imprisonment) and for Camões (sickness and death in an almshouse)? What we have here at least (though it is also something more and different, I would suggest) is Melville's rather pure and uncritical application to himself (revealed indirectly) of the romantic view of the artist woefully and ungraciously misused and abused by his society.

This view of Melville, or one similar to it, has of course been the historical view of Melville that has prevailed in the twentieth century. In fact, the strong desire to believe in the historicity of this view stands behind the continuing refusal by many readers to acknowledge the fact that Melville's works were not entirely ignored during the latter decades of his life or that they were not absolutely forgotten in the three decades following his death. That in the 1890s alone there were available various inexpensive editions of his major fiction (including *Moby-Dick*), and that they were advertised, noticed, and sold, is a fact that is itself ignored.

Since Melville held this Romantic-Renaissance conception of himself so late in life, that information must be factored into biographical accounts of those last years. What did it mean to him and what should it mean to his late twentieth-century readers that in his final years Herman Melville rationalized and aggrandized his self-perceived situation as a "failed writer"? Did it somehow enable that last collection of poems he was working on at the time of his death as well as the unfinished *Billy Budd*?

By way of a grace note to this discussion, there is something to be said, at least in passing, for including Jorge de Sena, the twentieth-century Portuguese writer, in this discussion of Camões, Tasso, and Melville. Sena makes numerous references to Tasso throughout his voluminous studies of Camões and the traditions of fifteenth-century literature, and he even translated Tasso's sonnet on Camões, publishing it first in his 1972 anthology of world poetry, *Poesia de 26 Séculos*,[69] and then in the November 1972 issue of the journal *Ocidente* devoted to Camões.[70] Of Tasso and Camões, Sena said once, "it was not without reason that the former died mad, just as the latter died of little more than hunger."[71] Indeed in 1964, Jorge de Sena had written "Super Flumina Babylonis," a narrative that takes as its theme Camões's last days.[72]

Sena was well aware that Melville was an admirer of Camões. In an entry on the Portuguese poet in the fifteenth edition of the *Encyclopaedia Britannica* (1974) Sena observes: "The Italian poet Torquato Tasso's sonnet to him [Camões] and the admiring quotations by the Spanish writer Baltasar Gracián in his *Agudeza y Arte de Ingenio* (1648) are examples of his fame, which was also noted by the Spanish dramatist Lope de Vega and poets Góngora, Milton, Goethe, the German Romantics, Byron, the Brownings, and others among his admirers, the last, but not the least, being Herman Melville."[73]

On 11 June 1961, the day after Camões Day, an event celebrated annually in various parts of the Portuguese-speaking world, Sena, like Melville decades earlier, adopted the voice of Camões for a first-person historical poem in which the angry poet delivers himself of a philippic against all mediocrities who now oppose him as well as those who will oppose him in the future.[74] In "Camões dirige-se aos seus contemporâneos" ("Camões Addresses His Contemporaries"), Sena writes:

Podereis roubar-me tudo:
as ideias, as palavras, as imagens,
e também as metáforas, os temas, os motivos,
os símbolos, e a primazia
nas dores sofridas de uma língua nova,
no entendimento de outros, na coragem
de combater, julgar, de penetrar
em recessos de amor para que sois castrados.
E podereis depois não me citar,
suprimir-me, ignorar-me, aclamar até
outros ladrões mais felizes.
Não importa nada: que o castigo
será terrivel. Não só quando
vossos netos não souberem já quem sois
terão de me saber melhor ainda
do que fingis que não sabeis,
como tudo, tudo o que laboriosamente pilhais,
reverterá para o meu nome. E mesmo será meu,
tido por meu, contado como meu,
até mesmo aquele pouco e miserável
que, só por vós, sem roubo, haveríeis feito.
Nada tereis, mas nada: nem os ossos,
que um vosso esqueleto há-de ser buscado,
para passar por meu. E para outros ladrões,
iguais a vós, de joelhos, porem flores no túmulo.

(Rob me blind:
My ideas, words, images,
Metaphors too, themes, motives,
Symbols, and the primacy
In feeling the pains of a new language,
In the understanding of others,
The courage to fight, judge, and to
Penetrate into the recesses of that
Love for which you are castrated.
And then you shall fail to acknowledge me,
Suppress me, ignore me, even acclaim
Other more fortunate thieves.
No great matter, for the punishment
Will be terrible. Not only when your
Grandchildren no longer know you
Will they have to know me better even than
That which you pretend not to know, for
All, all that you so laboriously steal,
Shall revert to my ownership. And
Even that will be mine, taken for
My property, counted as mine, those
Small and miserly things that you,
Without robbing them, have done.
You shall have nothing, nothing at all—
Not your very bones, for even one of your skeletons
Shall be fetched
And passed off for mine so that other
Thieves, your peers, will on their knees
Bring flowers to the tomb.)[75]

Sena himself, again like Melville, saw grand similarities between his own difficult circumstances and likely fate and those
of Camões.[76] While it is not certain that Sena actually knew
Melville's poem "Camoëns," there is no denying that there are
tantalizing similarities between his poem and Melville's. Three
quarters of a century after Melville's example Sena had done
exactly what the American had done. He had, like Melville before him (and Tasso before Melville), chosen to cast his biographical life along the mythic-legendary-literary lines of the
paradigm of powerful achievement followed first by neglect and
then by posthumous honor that Camões's putative life had first

made available to them all. In *Calamities of Authors* (1812) Isaac Disraeli writes about this paradigm, ending with an ironic question that might have been asked by any one of them—Camões, Tasso, Melville, Sena (even Mickle):

> Shall we account, among the lesser Calamities of Literature, that of a man of genius dedicating his days to the composition of a voluminous and national work, and when that labour is accomplished, the hope of fame, perhaps other hopes as necessary to reward past toil, and open to future enterprize, are all annihilated, or the unfinished work interrupted—on its publication? Yet this work neglected, or not relished, perhaps even the sport of witlings, afterwards is placed among the treasures of our language, when the Author is no more! but what is posthumous gratitude, could it reach even the ear of an angel?[77]

In 1867, a full decade after the publication of what would turn out to be his last published novel, *The Confidence-Man*, Melville rediscovered Camões. In May of that year he acquired his copy of Strangford's *Poems, from the Portuguese of Luis de Camoens* in the 1824 edition. For Melville, who had years earlier read this translation, it was a matter of renewing and reaffirming an old interest. What he might not have expected, however, was that the work, in certain respects, would relate to his own situation at the time. Of more than coincidental interest is the close proximity of the date on which Melville acquired this copy of Camões's *Poems* in the Strangford edition and—as discovered more than a century later—the date of Elizabeth Shaw Melville's tentative machinations to bring about a legal separation from her writer-husband. For it was on 17 May 1867 that Melville inscribed and dated his copy of *Poems, from the Portuguese*, eleven days after Elizabeth's half-brother wrote to the minister of New York City's All Souls Unitarian Church about Elizabeth Shaw Melville's marital difficulties with her husband.

Samuel Shaw's letter to the Reverend Henry Whitney Bellows spells out how Mrs. Melville might extricate herself from her marriage:

> The whole family understands the case and the thing has resolved itself into the mere question of my sisters willingness to

say the word. . . . If I understand your letter it is proposed to make a sudden interference and carry her off, she protesting that she does not wish to go and that it is none of her doing. But I think that this would only obscure the real merits of the case in the eyes of the world, of which she has a most exaggerated dread. . . .

The simplest way and the best way seems to me to be the one often talked about and once resolved upon viz that she should come to Boston as if on a visit, which would give her ample opportunity for preparation without exciting premature suspicion, and that when here her friends should inform her husband that a separation, for the present at least, has been decided on. That it should *not* appear to be the work of persons who urge her against her inclination but the deliberate decision of her judgement, which everybody believes to be good, assisted by the counsel of friends, and the professional advice of Dr. Gardner.

But if *we* are to seem to be the real putters asunder of man and wife and she is merely to acquiesce I do not think it could be managed better than by having her at our house and by keeping her there and carefully preventing her husband from seeing her, and telling him and everybody that we had made up our minds not to let her return.

But this might embarrass our subsequent relations with Mr. Melville and really injure my sisters case because if he should commence legal proceedings it would throw suspicion over her motives in acquiescing in a separation.

It may well be said Here is a case of mischief making where the wifes relations have created all the trouble. "She says *now* that her husband ill treated her so that she could not live with him but why did she not say so before. She goes to Boston and by dint of argument and remonstrances and bad advice of all sorts is at last persuaded into thinking herself a much injured woman." &c &c &c

And her very patience and fortitude will be turned into arguments against her belief in the insanity of her husband.

I think that the safest course is to let her real position become apparent from the first, namely that of a wife, who, being convinced that her husband is insane *acts* as if she were so convinced and applies for aid and assistance to her friends and acts *with* them.[78]

Elizabeth wished, clearly, to end a bad marriage to a husband whose insanity, it was claimed, was not a recent development, according to Samuel Shaw's letter to Henry Whitney Bellows (6 May 1867), which has just been quoted at length, and Elizabeth's own follow-up letter to Henry Whitney Bellows (20 May 1867). The execution of the proposed plan called for great secrecy, however. It must need be carried out in such a way that Melville would suspect nothing until the separation—with Elizabeth initially going off to Boston on a family visit to put it all in motion—were a *fait accompli*. The plan fell through, however, and the Melvilles remained together. Just how much Melville knew or suspected of Elizabeth's attitude toward him at this time, of her judgment regarding his sanity, and of her decision to seek out the best means of separating from him, cannot be known for certain.

That he might not have been totally in the dark, however, is suggested by what he chose to mark, presumably at this time, in Strangford's translation of Camões. For on 17 May 1867, as Jay Leyda notes, Melville scored "two passages in Strangford's introduction and one in Camões' Sonnet VI."[79] Leyda does not say, though, that there are other Melville markings in the book, a failure that might lead one to infer, erroneously, that there were only three such markings. But for the moment we shall consider only the three markings indicated by Leyda, reserving our consideration of the others, which, incidentally, have never figured in any Melville scholarship that I know of.

Significantly, the subject of those lines Leyda notes as having been scored by Melville in Camões's poem, the opening three, is "Reason" and madness. Of particular interest is the poet's assertion that his self-imposed isolation has led "the crowd" to judge him insane:

> My senses lost, misjudging men declare,
> And Reason banish'd from her mental throne,
> Because I shun the crowd, and dwell alone . . .[80]

In Strangford's introduction Melville scored two discrete passages, one on public taste and political decay, and a second on the faithful ministrations of womankind: "So true it is, that the decline of public spirit in matters of taste is a certain indication of political decay,"[81] and "Woman was to him [Camões] as a ministering angel, and for the little joy which he tasted in life, he was indebted to her."[82]

Brian Head notes that of three passages in Strangford scored by Melville (like virtually everyone else at the time, he did not know that there were other scorings), the first from the introduction and the lines from the poetry were of special significance to Melville. The third passage, referring to "Woman," he sees as less important. Since "Love is not one of the favorite themes of Melville," writes Head, "his identification with Camoens during the latter phase of his life is in terms of similarity in disillusionment rather than in treatments of the theme of love."[83]

Yet it can be argued that Melville's scoring of the passage in Strangford's introduction on the way in which Camões, characteristically following Petrarch, viewed women in the most adulatory terms is of an importance equal, at least, to that of those passages referring to the decline in public taste and the bitterness of public judgments of Camões's insanity. Given what we now know of Elizabeth Shaw Melville's attitude toward her husband in May 1867, at the very time he acquired Strangford's *Poems, from the Portuguese,* and of her abortive stratagems for leaving him, we might be warranted in deciding that Melville saw how ironically those passages applied to his own experience. Faced both with public disdain for his work and the growing charge of madness that he shared across the centuries with the Portuguese epic poet, Melville could surely identify with Camões—but only to a point. In this sense it is important that he scored not only its first three lines but lines six through eleven as well; yet every line of the whole of Camões's "Sonnet VI" (Strangford's translation and numbering) can be seen to pertain to Melville's situation in May 1867:

> My senses lost, misjudging men declare,
>> And Reason banish'd from her mental throne,
>> Because I shun the crowd, and dwell alone
> In the calm trance of undisturb'd despair,
> Tears all my pleasure—all my comfort care!

> But I have known, from long experience known
> How vain the worship to those idols shown,
> Which charm the world, and reign unrivall'd there:
> Proud dreams of pow'r and fortune's gilded glare,
> The lights that blaze in tall Ambition's tow'r,
> For such, let others waste life's little hour
> In toil and weary search—but be it mine,
> Lady! to muse of thee—and in my bow'r
> Pour to thy praise the soul-impassion'd line![84]

If Melville could identify with the Camões that "misjudging men" had deemed insane and who had long since renounced the world of "proud dreams of pow'r, and fortune's gilded glare," he could not comfort himself, as Camões had, with the thought of devoting himself to composing "soul-impassioned" poetry to his Lady. To have line-scored the remaining three lines of "Sonnet VI" would merely have served to call attention still again to the irony he had marked in Strangford's introduction when he scored the passage: "Woman was to him [Camões] as a ministering angel, and for the little joy which he tasted in life, he was indebted to her."[85]

It is not surprising, therefore, that Melville would later write his two-part poem "Camoëns" and that in that poem he should eschew Camões's high tribute to his Lady and his unwavering confidence in the benevolent ministrations of womankind. One can readily draw the parallels between Melville's painful circumstances and those of Camões, particularly when Melville writes:

> Exhausted by the exacting lay,
> Thou dost but fall a surer prey
> To wile and guile ill understood;
> While they who work them, fair in face,
> Still keep their strength in prudent place,
> And claim they worthier run life's race,
> Serving high God with useful good.[86]

It would not do to apply these lines to the Camões whose fealty to womankind appears never to have faltered. It would do nicely, however, to see in them Melville's own disguised judgment of Elizabeth Shaw Melville's role in his own fall to low estate in

40

MADRIGAL.   *(V. N.)*
(Spanish.)

———

" *Mi coraçon me han roubado*
  Y Amor viendo mis enojos," &c.

———

THE heart that warm'd my guileless breast
  Some wanton hand had thence convey'd,
But Love, who saw his bard distress'd,
  In pity thus the thief betray'd—
" 'Tis she who owns the fairest mien
  And sweetest eyes that e'er were seen !"

And sure if Love be in the right,
  (And was Love ever in the wrong ?)
To thee, my first and sole delight,
  That simple heart must now belong—
Because thou hast the fairest mien
And sweetest eyes that e'er were seen !

X *Mrs Browning's verses on this.*

A page from Melville's
copy of Lord Viscount
Strangford's *Poems,*
from the Portuguese
of Luis de Camoens.

1867. If it is true, as we know it is, that later decades brought about a remarkable change for the better in Melville's relations with his wife, it is nevertheless most likely that the latter 1860s marked the nadir of their emotional estrangement.

What now—to return to Melville's copy of the 1824 edition of Strangford's translation of Camões's lyric poems—is to be made of Melville's other markings? Some of them are more significant to our purpose than others, of course, but none of them is without interest. One "Madrigal," for example, Melville marked in two ways and in two places. He inserted a triple check, always a sign of high approval or great interest, at the beginning of the poem, and he underlined all but the first word in the last line of the first stanza.

And *sweetest eyes that e'er were seen!*[87]

He also placed an "**x**" at the left of the line to key it to his annotation at the bottom of the page, which reads: "Mrs Browning's verses on this." Camões's poem is a love poem, but its importance for Melville lay less in its expressed sentiments, apparently, than in the fact that he had recognized the source for Elizabeth Barrett Browning's own tribute to the Portuguese poet, the poem "Catarina to Camoëns," first published in 1843.

Of a second "Madrigal" Melville chose to line-score in the left margin the poem's opening two lines, which seem to have brought him back nostalgically to his years on the high seas. "Dear is the blush of early light," Camões the sailor had written, "To him who ploughs the pathless deep."[88] Melville, the old sailor, now land-locked in the New York Custom House, responded with an insider's recognition. That Melville might well have been comparing his present situation with those of earlier and, in retrospect, better times is indicated by the fact that the next poem in the volume that called for marking was "Sonnet VI," which, as we have already noted, begins, "My senses lost, misjudging men declare, / And Reason banish'd from her mental throne."

Melville triple-checked three other sonnets, and all three sound the note of loss and pain: "Sonnet VIII" on the Mondego river, "Sonnet XII" on the death of Antonio Noronha, and "Sonnet XVII" on the lost stuff of remembered dreams. First, "Sonnet VIII."

> Mondego! thou, whose waters cold and clear
>   Gird those green banks, where Fancy fain would stay,
>   Fondly to muse on that departed day
> When Hope was kind and Friendship seem'd sincere;
> —Ere I had purchas'd knowledge with a tear.
>   —Mondego! though I bend my pilgrim way
>   To other shores, where other fountains stray,
> And other rivers roll their proud career,
> Still—nor shall time, nor grief, nor stars severe,
>   Nor widening distance e'er prevail in aught
> To make thee less to this sad bosom dear;
>   And Memory oft, by old Affection taught,
>   Shall lightly speed upon the plumes of thought,
> To bathe amongst thy waters cold and clear![89]

The poem elegizes that "departed day / When Hope was kind and Friendship seem'd sincere." It is the Mondego and the poet's memories of its "waters cold and clear" that will remain dear to the poet when, as Melville, who was deep in familial disintegration, was even then experiencing, that Hope was no longer kind and Friendship no longer even "seem'd" sincere.

One need not accept the notion promulgated by some biographers that Melville was enamored of Nathaniel Hawthorne to recognize that Melville did express strong feelings for other men.[90] The attractions of male comrades appear everywhere in his fiction, from *Typee* (Toby Greene), *White-Jacket* (Jack Chase), *Moby-Dick* (Ishmael and Queequeg) to the cheery denizens of that London "Paradise of Bachelors" and, in the tragic mode, to *Billy Budd*.[91] One wonders, moreover, if in 1867 Camões's celebration of the memory of his "dear lost Antonio" would not have been particularly poignant to a man sensitive to what he felt had been his recent betrayal by the woman who was his wife. Camões's poem on Antonio de Noronha, dead in a battle with the Moors in 1553, reads:

> Dear lost Antonio! whilst I yet deplore
>   My bosom's friend—and mourn the withering blow
>   Which laid, in manly flow'r, the warrior low,
> Whose valour sham'd the glorious deeds of yore;
> E'en while mine eyes their humid tribute pour,
>   My spirit feels a sad delight, to know
>   That thou hast but resign'd a world of woe
> For one, where pains and griefs shall wound no more;
>   Tho' torn, alas, from this sublunar sphere,
> For ever torn, by War's ungentle hand,
>   Still, were the Muse but as Affection strong,
>   My dead Antonio should revive in song,
> And, grac'd by Poetry's "melodious tear,"
> Live, in the memory of a grateful land![92]

One last poem, "Sonnet XVII," earned Melville's final triple-check. In this instance, besides the check, the engaged reader decisively underscored the poem's final line, "They charm a moment—and they are no more"! "They" refers sadly and pain-

fully to "the thousand thoughts of yore." From the beginning
the poem builds to that last line.

> From sorrow free, and tears, and dull despair,
>   I liv'd contented in a sweet repose;
>   I heeded not the happier star of those
> Whose amorous wiles achiev'd each conquer'd fair;
> (Such bliss I deem'd full dearly bought with care:)
>   Mine was meek Love, that ne'er to frenzy rose,
>   And for its partners in my soul I chose
> Benevolence, that never dreamt a snare,
> And Independence, proudly cherish'd there!
> —Dead now is Happiness—'tis past, 'tis o'er—
>   And in its place, the thousand thoughts of yore,
> Which haunt my melancholy bosom, seem
> Like the faint memory of a pleasing dream—
>   They charm a moment—and they are no more![93]

"They charm a moment—and they are no more!"—Melville had
bottomed out in 1867.

One last sentence on Camões and Melville. Whatever colors
the Melvillean spirit chose, or was forced to wear—whether they
were the reds and greens inspired by the epic challenge of the
Camões who wrote *Os Lusíadas* or the dark and somber hues
of the Camões who, in disrepute and disgrace, struggled in his
lyric poetry to put the shards of his life back together—Camões
was ever, to Melville, the poet and the man for all seasons.

6

Longfellow's Taste

No American writer's life could have been more different from Melville's than that of Henry Wadsworth Longfellow. Surely, he had no need to lament his fate, for his popularity and reputation was intact at the time of his death in 1882. He felt no need, as Melville did, to write poems about the great neglected poets such as Tasso and Camões. Indeed, at the time of his death there was no more famous or esteemed poet in the United States than the author of *Evangeline* (1847), *Hiawatha* (1855), *The Courtship of Miles Standish* (1858), and several universally admired lyrics.

For nearly a quarter of a century Longfellow was also a college and university teacher, serving as professor and librarian at Bowdoin College (1829-1835) and, later, distinguishing himself as Smith Professor of French and Spanish at Harvard University (1836-1854). Finding a lack of suitable textbooks and language readers, especially in his first years teaching, he set about providing them himself. By 1830 he had written, constructed, and shepherded through the press four textbooks: *Elements of French Grammar*, *French Exercises*, *Manuel de Proverbes Dramatiques*, and *Novelas Españolas*. These were followed in 1833 by *Syllabus de la Grammaire Italienne* and *Saggi de' Novellieri Italiani d'Ogni Secolo*. In time he became a contributor to the *North American Review* of learned essays on the languages and literatures of France, Spain, Italy, and Portugal. From the Spanish he translated the *Coplas de Manrique* to which he appended a professorial essay on the moral and devotional poetry of Spain.[1]

Longfellow's scholarly interests extended beyond the languages and literatures of southern Europe, however. He knew a good deal about the literatures of Scandinavia and Germany, for example, which led him to embark on an ambitious project of disseminating European poetry through the medium of the anthology. In 1845 he published *The Poets and Poetry of Europe*, an oversized volume presenting generous selections of work from ten countries, accompanied by extensive scholarly essays, and between 1876 and 1879 he brought out in thirty-one small volumes *Poems of Places*—"a kind of poetical gazeteer,"[2]—the making of which he described as "a pleasant occupation . . ., travelling in one's easy chair, and making one's own poetic guide-book."[3] Newton Arvin, Longfellow's best twentieth-century critic, characterizes this "extraordinarily ambitious project": "There is the usual mingling, in these volumes, of good, mediocre, and bad poems, but whatever else may be said of *Poems of Places*, its comprehensiveness can hardly be called into question. . . . The sense of place has, at least, never been anthologized more thoroughly."[4]

It is not known just when Longfellow thought of the idea for *The Poets and Poetry of Europe*. He appears to have begun work on this immense work in the fall of 1843. An early reference to the project comes in a letter on 12 January 1844 to his brother Samuel, then serving in Faial as tutor to the children of Charles Dabney, longtime United States Consul at the Azores: "I am publishing a book, a collection of translations from various languages, to the number of 10, the translations by various hands—and a few by my own. If you have found anything pretty in the Portuguese, pray let me have it. Have you translated any thing yet? Dont neglect this opportunity of learning the language thoroughly. You ought to speak it muito bem [very well] by this time. How much longer shall you stay in Fayal?"[5] Less than a year and a half later, in June 1845, *The Poets and Poetry of Europe* was brought out by Metcalf and Company in Cambridge. Later in the year the Philadelphia publisher Carey and Hart stereotyped it, printing it again in 1847 and 1849. In the next five years there were an additional three reprints in Philadelphia alone. A measure of the success of this anthology is that the total number of reprints in the period 1845-1896 was at least ten.[6] "Nothing like *The Poets and Poetry of Europe* had ever appeared before, here or in England," concludes Arvin, "and one doubts whether anything like it had ever appeared on the Continent."[7]

From the beginning, Longfellow intended to include Portugal among the ten countries represented in his anthology. "The languages from which translations are here presented," he wrote, "[include] the six Gothic languages of the North of Europe,—Anglo-Saxon, Icelandic, Danish, Swedish, German, and Dutch; and the four Latin languages of the South of Europe,—French, Italian, Spanish, and Portuguese."[8] When his publisher objected to the length of the book, suggesting apparently that the section on Portuguese poetry be shortened or, perhaps, even eliminated altogether, Longfellow defended his decisions. "I am sorry to find, that the 'Poets and Poetry of Europe' over-runs a little the 750 pages," he wrote. "You must not be alarmed at this; for in such a work *completeness* is a great thing; and the Portuguese Poetry being rather a rare and curious portion of the work, I could not bear to cut it off too short."[9] In sticking to his guns on this matter, Longfellow was tacitly opposing such easy "facts" as the one expressed anonymously in the *North American Review* a few years earlier: "the Portuguese literature is properly an appendage and constituent part of the same Peninsular school" as the Spanish.[10] Longfellow knew the argument of J.C.L. Simonde de Sismondi, who in the *Historical View of the Literature of the South of Europe* devotes a large portion of volume four of his work to Portuguese literature, explaining:

> Portugal . . . possesses a literature of its own; and its language, so far from being ranked as a mere dialect of the Spanish, was regarded by an independent people as the characteristic of their freedom, and was cultivated with proportional assiduity and delight. Hence the most celebrated among the Portuguese devoted their talents to confer lustre on the literary character of their country, emulating each other in every species of excellence, in order that their neighbours might, in no branch whatever, boast of any advantage over them. This national spirit has given to their productions a character quite distinct from the Castilian.[11]

Longfellow won his battle with his publisher.

He introduced his section on Portuguese poetry with a five-page, double-columned essay entitled "Portuguese Language and Poetry." Of Camões he wrote eloquently, availing himself of the most dramatic and romantic accounts of the poet's life and death then current:

> [T]he greatest poet of the sixteenth century, as of all others in Portuguese poetry, is he who sang of
>
> > "the renowned men,
> > Who, from the western Lusitanian shore,
> > Sailing through seas man never sailed before,
> > Passed beyond Taprobane,"—
>
> Luis de Camoens, author of the national epic, "Os Lusíadas," who lived in poverty and wretchedness, died in the Lisbon hospital, and, after death, was surnamed the Great,—a title never given before, save to popes and emperors. The life of no poet is so full of vicissitude and romantic adventure as that of Camoens. In youth, he was banished from Lisbon on account of a love affair with Catharina de Attayda, a *dama do paço*, or lady of honor at court; he served against the Moors as a volunteer on board the fleet in the Mediterranean, and lost his right eye by a gun-shot wound in a battle off Ceuta; he returned to Lisbon, proud and poor, but found no favor at court, and no means of a livelihood in the city; he abandoned his native land for India, indignantly exclaiming with Scipio, "*Ingrata patria, non possidebis ossa mea!*" three ships of the squadron were lost in a storm, he reached Goa safely in the fourth; he fought under the king of Cochin against the king of Pimenta; he fought against the Arabian corsairs in the Red Sea; he was banished from Goa to the island of Macao, where he became administrator of the effects of deceased persons, and where he wrote the greater part of the "Lusiad"; he was shipwrecked on the coast of Camboya, saving only his life and his poem, the manuscript of which he brought ashore saturated with sea-water; he was accused of malversation in office, and thrown into prison at Goa; after an absence of sixteen years, he returned in abject poverty to Lisbon, then ravaged by the plague; he lived a few years on a wretched pension granted him by King Sebastian when the "Lusiad" was published, and on the alms which a slave he had brought with him from India collected at night in the streets of Lisbon; and finally died in the hospital, exclaiming, "Who could believe that on so small a stage as that of one poor bed Fortune would choose to represent so great a tragedy?" Thus was completed the Iliad of his woes. Fifteen years

afterward, a splendid monument was erected to his memory; so that, as has been said of another, "he asked for bread, and they gave him a stone."[12]

Of the thirty-some pages Longfellow devoted to Portuguese poetry itself, nine of them (along with three and a half columns of further commentary on the work)—by far the most allotted to any one poet—were given over to work by Camões.[13] He was represented by twenty-two items: two extracts from *Os Lusíadas*, eleven sonnets, and nine lyrics. Not one of the translations was by Longfellow. True to his word, both in the Portuguese section and elsewhere, he had "attempted only to bring together, into a compact and convenient form, as large an amount as possible of those English translations which are scattered through many volumes, and are not easily accessible to the general reader."[14]

In this mid–nineteenth-century anthology, constructed in the midst of a period of American romanticism, flourishing a little later than English romanticism, Longfellow is receptive to the two Camões. He remembers the epic poet by choosing and printing excerpts from William Julius Mickle's translation, *The Lusiad; or, The Discovery of India* (1776), extracting sections from *Os Lusíadas*, including the "Spirit of the Cape" section, which had inspired the monsters in Joel Barlow's *The Columbiad* and in Edgar Allan Poe's *Pym*. He attends to the lyric Camões with a generous sampling of his shorter poetry. From Strangford's *Poems, from the Portuguese of Luis de Camoens* he takes eight lyrics ("Lembrevos minha tristeza," "Quando o sol encuberto vay mostrando," "Sepa, quien padece," "Tiempo! que todo mudas," "Eu cantey, jâ, e agora," "Não nos engane a riqueza," "Os bõs vi sempre passar," and "Segreda noite Amiga, a que obedeço") and three sonnets ("O culto divinal se celebrava," "A fermosura desta fresca serra," and "Os olhos onde o casto Amor ardia").[15] From Felicia Hemans's widely read collection *Translations from Camoens* (1818) he reprints five sonnets ("Já a saudosa Aurora destoucava," "Alma minha gentil," "Moradoras gentis e delicadas," "Delegadas, claras águas do Mondego," and "Como quando do mar tempestuoso").[16] And, finally, from Thomas Roscoe's translation of the *Historical View of the Literature of the South of Europe*, he collects three sonnets ("No mundo poucos anos, e cansados," "Que me quereis, perpétuas saudades," "Que poderei do undo, já querer," and lines from one song "Canção X," beginning "A piedade humana me faltava").[17]

Yet despite this generous attention to Camões the lyric poet, Longfellow betrays clearly that he personally values Camões's epic poetry more highly, placing it on the first pages, even though most of the poet's lyrical poetry was composed earlier than *Os Lusíadas*. In this regard Longfellow's preference accords with the general tastes of his time, which honored the "large" poem over the "smaller" poem—the epic over the lyric—and is in sure if implicit disagreement with Edgar Allan Poe's notion that there exists no such thing as the "long" poem. "What we term a long poem is, in fact, merely a succession of brief ones—that is to say, of brief poetical effects," writes Poe. "For this reason, at least one half of the 'Paradise Lost' is essentially prose—a succession of poetical excitements interspersed, *inevitably*, with corresponding depressions."[18] The poet of *The Song of Hiawatha*, *Evangeline: A Tale of Acadie*, and the undervalued *Christus: A Mystery*, as well as the translator of the *Divina Commedia*, obviously, for all of his own shorter poems—lyric, narrative, sonnet—preferred the poetry of the large canvas. It may be no more than coincidental, but even Longfellow's *obiter dicta*—remarks made in later decades—about Camões's work refer to *Os Lusíadas*.

When he assembled his *Poems of Places*, the multi-volume work published in Boston by Houghton Mifflin in 1876-1879, Longfellow went largely to the same sources for his translations of Camões. There, in volume fifteen, the second volume entitled *Spain &c.*, he included a section of poems about Portugal. Here again he reprinted W.J. Mickle's version of the "Ignez de Castro" episode, along with his separate sections entitled "Lusitania," "The Complaint of Camoens," and "Lisbon." The sonnet "Claras agoas e frias do Mondego," entitled now "Mondego, the River," he took from Strangford. "Moradoras gentis e delicadas," now called "The River Tagus," came from Felicia Hemans. "Cancão IV" ("Vão as serenas aguas") called simply "Coimbra," and "Elegia III" ("O Sulmonense Ovidio desterrado,") entitled "Elegy Written in Banishment at Santarem," are attributed to Mrs. Cockle, who versified John Adamson's prose translations.[19] And "Vão as serenas águas"— also called "Mondego"—was credited to William Herbert.[20]

Longfellow's interest in Camões had a long history. As early as 1832 he agreed to a project that would have involved Camões, the preparation of "an Article on the Spanish and Portuguese languages for some future No. of the N.A.R. [*North American Review*]."[21] Documentation of his knowledge of Camões is scanty, however. In his earliest reference to the Portuguese poet, in 1840, he relates the essentials of the story of "the spirit of the cape": "It is told by Camoens in his Lusiad that when the Giant Adamastor tried to embrace the sea-nymph Thetis, she slipped away, and he embraced the shaggy Cape of Good-hope."[22] Thirty-five years later, he writes to James E. Hewitt:

> I have had the pleasure of receiving the specimen of your translation of the Lusiad, and hasten to thank you for your kindness in sending it to me.
>
> I have read it with great satisfaction. You have made an excellent beginning; and I am particularly delighted that you preserve the stanzas of the original and do not attempt to recast the poem into another form. This Mickle did, and almost destroyed the identity of the work. Form is so much in poetry![23]

In 1877 Longfellow was in the midst of bringing out *Poems of Places*. In his correspondence for that year there occur a handful of casual references to Camões. On 3 May, to a Portuguese correspondent, Jayme Batalha Reis, he writes again to thank him for the "beautiful and very welcome present of the 'Obras de Camões,'" explaining that he had written the previous week, but "not having your address I directed my letter to the Centennial Exhibition Grounds in Philadelphia."[24] A few weeks later, in July, Batalha Reis visited Longfellow in Cambridge, Massachusetts.[25]

The criticism of Mickle's translation of *Os Lusíadas* that Longfellow voiced in the letter to Hewitt quoted above, he intensified in a letter to Moses Woolson, the proprietor of a school in Concord, New Hampshire. On 26 September 1877 he writes:

There are three English translations of Camoens' "Lusiad";
one by Richard Fanshaw [London, 1655]; a Second by [Will-
iam] Julius Mickle [Oxford, 1776]; and the third by Thos. Moore
Musgrave [London, 1826].

Of these the best known is that of Mickle; but it is rather
a paraphrase than a translation. Two extracts from it may be
found in "The Poets and Poetry of Europe," a work edited by
me some years ago.

These extracts, "Ignez de Castro" and "The Spirit of the
Cape" [both of which are given in Mickle's translation in
Longfellow's *The Poets and Poetry of Europe*] are the most celebrated passages of the poem; and either of them would answer your purpose. Of the two I rather prefer the latter.[26]

Woolson's "purpose" was a proposed lecture by Mrs. Woolson,
in which she hoped to incorporate a passage from Camões.

Among Longfellow's admirers from abroad no one was more
famous than Dom Pedro II. The Emperor of Brazil was not only
an avid reader of the American's poetry but one of its translators. On Christmas Day in 1877 Longfellow wrote to Dom Pedro.
Once again he turned to the subject of Mickle's translation: "I
have had occasion lately to look into Mickle's translation of the
Lusiad. It is easily and gracefully versified, but properly speaking is not a translation, but a very free paraphrase, or *rifacimento*
of the original. I have been amazed to find what long passages
of his own the writer has interpolated into the work. He does
not even follow the division into stanzas, but recasts the whole
into English couplets. This, to me, is a fatal error."[27] Then
Longfellow switches to a different matter, James Edwin Hewitt's
translation of Camões, though he cannot remember the
translator's name. He writes: "I am sorry that I have lost and
cannot recover the name of the young Englishman at Rio, of
whom I spoke to you as being engaged in making a new version of the famous poem. I am confident, that a word of interest from you would be a great encouragement to him in his
arduous task. The portion of his work, which he sent me had
very decided merits."[28] Hewitt's work—cantos one and two of
Os Lusíadas—was not published in book form until 1883, when
it appeared in Rio de Janeiro, though Hewitt had in 1880 published canto one in *The British and American Mail*, the Rio de

Janeiro publication of which he was editor, as part of the tricentenary celebration in Brazil.[29]

Something should be said about Longfellow's repeated reservations in the 1870s about Mickle's translation of *Os Lusíadas*. He had of course been silent in the matter when he anthologized the "Ignez de Castro" and "Spirit of the Cape" episodes in *The Poets and Poetry of Europe* in 1845 and his reservations in 1877 did not keep him from including the latter in *Poems of Places* in the same year, even though presumably he could have gone back to Fanshawe's 1655 version. Oddly, although he could have leveled the same charge against Strangford's translations of Camões—that he had paraphrased and expanded—he for some reason did not. It will be recalled that the English poet Robert Southey, with strong credentials as a student of Portuguese literature and history, had immediately upon their publication objected to Strangford's translations, suggesting that the Viscount, thinking "Camoens too low," had sought to raise "him upon stilts."[30] Strangford, no less than Mickle, fell short of the standard Longfellow, himself a distinguished translator, set for such work: "That translation is best which combines most of the spirit, form, phrase of the original."[31]

Longfellow's copy of Strangford's *Poems, from the Portuguese of Luis de Camoens* has survived. Published in Philadelphia by H. Maxwell in 1805 and carrying the signature "H. W. Longfellow," this copy is now at Harvard University's Houghton Library. The copy is lightly marked and "corrected" throughout—marginal line scorings, penciled-in small and large x's, an underlining or two. It is most probable that Longfellow used this copy when he was preparing *The Poets and Poetry of Europe* and, later, *Poems of Places*, but there is no indication that he was disappointed with Strangford's versions as translations or that he recognized what Southey did when he wrote of Viscount Strangford that "his Lordship has fathered his own verses upon Camoens."[32]

Re-published as late as 1896, *The Poets and Poetry of Europe* was still performing its "genuinely Arnoldian role," as Arvin says, "in helping to propagate among American readers 'the best that is known and thought in the world,'" when Ezra Pound coupled

Longfellow's name with that of Camões.[33] Of *Os Lusíadas* Longfellow had written:

> Besides the "Lusiad," Camoens wrote sonnets, songs, odes, elegies, eclogues, *redondilhas*, epigrams, epistles, and three comedies. They all exhibit an exalted genius, and the noblest traits of character. But his great national epic, the "Lusiad," is the crowning glory of his life, and the highest literary claim that his country has to urge upon the respect of foreign nations. In it are immortalized the grand discoveries of Vasco da Gama, and the illustrious deeds that adorn the annals of the great age of Portugal,—the age of enthusiasm, adventure, and gigantic enterprise. In spirit and style it is more national than any other heroic poem of modern times; and notwithstanding the incongruities of the supernatural machinery, introduced by the poet in compliance with the pedantic views that prevailed in his age, it must be considered an admirable monument of genius. It displays great powers of invention, the most plastic command of style, and, at times, a wonderful sublimity of conception. Many passages are adorned with the most exquisite beauties and the most melting tenderness of sentiment, the richest music of language and the most glowing imagery. Above all, it is informed with the profound and impassioned feelings of the poet's heart.[34]

In *The Spirit of Romance* (1910) the young Ezra Pound takes his turn at assessing Camões's achievement in *Os Lusíadas*. Unlike Longfellow, he judges it rather severely.[35] In the course of his argument, however, Pound does a curious thing: he draws an extended comparison between the sixteenth-century Portuguese poet Camões and the nineteenth-century American poet Longfellow, attempting to demonstrate that milieu in both cases is responsible not just for the nature of their work but for its shared mediocrity. It is not on Pound's overall viewpoint that one must focus here, but on the choice he has made for his comparison. Ostensibly aiming his attack at Camões, Pound has doubled his pleasure by choosing to single out as a point of comparison one of the paragons of George Santayana's so-called genteel tradition. Yet the linking of Camões with Longfellow is less imaginative than fanciful, serving best to remind us that the young professional student of Romance languages and literatures was probably well acquainted, as were those Americans interested in poetry during Pound's formative years, with the selections Longfellow had made for his *Poets and Poetry of Europe*. At the turn of the century Longfellow was still leading the writers and teachers of Pound's generation to the great poets of Europe, including Camões.

7

Higginson and Dickinson Tributes

"She was much too enigmatical a being for me to solve in an hour's interview," recalled Thomas Wentworth Higginson several years after Emily Dickinson's death in 1886, "and an instinct told me that the slightest attempt to direct cross-examination would make her withdraw into her shell; I could only sit still and watch as one does in the woods; I must name my bird without a gun, as recommended by Emerson."[1] Yet, notwithstanding his bemusement before this rare creature of nature and despite his inability during her lifetime to accept as fully realized poetry "the beautiful thoughts and words" she sent him,[2] Higginson's own portion of literary fame in the twentieth century has rested largely on the single turn of fate that enabled him, during the last quarter century of Emily Dickinson's life, to serve as the virtually unpublished poet's "Preceptor" (her term) and, after her death, to become the co-editor (with Mabel Loomis Todd) of her first two volumes of poetry, *Poems* (1890) and *Poems, Second Series* (1891).

In his time he was a well-known public figure, one known for his views and deeds as an abolitionist, as a supporter of the women's movement, as a poet, critic, and essayist. But despite current attempts to accord him his modicum of historical prominence in those areas, he is still best known by far for his good offices in matters Dickinsonian—nurturing her emotional and spiritual life and contributing to those publications that furthered the public reception of her work and, subsequently, her burgeoning literary reputation.

For several months, over the winter of 1855-1856, Higginson lived in the Azores, on the island of Faial. He had accompanied his ailing young wife in her search for a more salubrious climate. During his stay, with a good deal of time on his hands, Higginson embarked on several projects, among them the study of the Portuguese language and the history and literature of Portugal. That study resulted rather promptly in a long essay, purporting to be an omnibus review of books dealing with matters Portuguese, for the *North American Review*. It appeared in October 1856, some four months after the Higginsons had returned to their home in Boston.

"Portugal's Glory and Decay," as Higginson sees Portugal's history, tells a doleful story of great historical achievement during the Age of the Discoveries when Portugal led Europe, followed by precipitous decline in national fortune brought about by military defeat and a devastating century of shipwreck. Out of that regrettable history, however, has emerged the luminous figure of Luis de Camões, about whom Higginson offers a detailed digression.

"The decay of the nation had begun, but not before it had made its mark upon literature as well as history. Those glories educated, that decline stimulated, the genius of Camoens. His life commenced in the year after the death of Albuquerque (1517), and ended in the year after the death of Sebastian (1579); thus spanning the interval between triumph and decline." Obviously drawing on the accounts of John Adamson, Lord Strangford, and (possibly) Longfellow, Higginson offers the standard romantic account of Camões's life.

> What a tragedy was the poet's own life meanwhile! Brave, generous, patient, laborious, accomplished, fascinating, he died sick, starving, forgotten; the defeat of Alçarquivir giving, it is thought, the last blow to his heroic spirit. His dying words were of sad rejoicing, that he perished with his country,—"*ao menos morro com ella.*" Fifteen years after, they wrote upon his tomb: "Here lies the prince among the poets of his age; he lived poor and miserable, and he died the same." Yet when this Camoens swam to the beach of Cochin-China, holding his poem above the waves in his hand, it was the renown of Portugal that he bore. What would his country have had remaining, if that hand had lost its grasp? But, at this day, Camoens is, to almost all, the shadow of a name. No wonder that it is so. Time has not, indeed, impaired the fame of Dante, any more than of the

greater Shakespeare; but the same cannot be said of Tasso and Ariosto, and how could Camoens, writing in a less known language a poem similar in structure to theirs, expect to escape their fate? Nay, there are no gondoliers to prolong the sweetness of his strain; no great astronomer, to attribute to him, as Galileo did to Ariosto, the perfect beauty of his own scientific style; no Professor Marsand, to collect a library of nine hundred commentaries, like the Bibliotheca Petrarchensis at Padua;—only the sad and patient Portuguese, clinging to their one poet, and waiting for another, as they waited for Sebastian. We have heard of the *homo unius libri*; here is a nation of one book.

And that book, continues Higginson (who had only recently studied Camões's language) is worthy of the tongue in which it is written.

[T]here are stately charms in the Lusiad, worthy of the sweet language in which it is written. It has the Italian graces,—beauty of melody, descriptive eloquence, and occasional fine touches of feeling. It is, to be sure, disfigured by a cumbrous mythology; yet perhaps its narration has a nobler interest than that of the Orlando or the Gierusalemme, even if it shows less skill of invention. Humboldt, in his Cosmos, has compared its descriptions of nature with theirs, and given the Portuguese epic the palm. Mickle has done for Camoens what Hoole did for the Italian poets,—the most, namely, that a feeble translator can do. But if the number of foreign versions gives fame, the Lusiad has it. It is said that there have been five complete translations into Italian, four into Spanish, four into French, four into German, three into English, and one each into Swedish, Danish, and Russian, to say nothing of six into Latin and one into Hebrew,—thirty in all.[3]

Camões makes another significant, albeit brief, appearance in Higginson's writing. He appears in "Letter to a Young Contributor," the piece in the *Atlantic Monthly* for April 1862 that caught Emily Dickinson's eye and which prompted her to address to him her first letter asking him for criticism of her work. Therein Higginson writes: "Literature is attar of roses, one distilled drop from a million blossoms. Think how Spain and Por-

tugal once divided the globe between them in a treaty, when
England was a petty kingdom of illiterate tribes!—and now all
Spain is condensed for us into Cervantes, and all Portugal into
the fading fame of the unread Camoens."[4] This reference would
not have been lost on Dickinson (little was lost on Dickinson),
especially not on the incipient poet who read and contributed
to *The Indicator*,[5] the Amherst College literary publication which,
as Barton Levi St. Armand affirms, served as "a source of obvious stimulus to Dickinson in the late 1840s."[6] In *The Indicator*
for June 1848, its very first issue, appeared an essay on Camões.
Dickinson would not have ignored this piece, especially its account of Camões's ill-fated love for "Dona Catharina de Atayde,
a lady of rare accomplishments"—an *"affair du coeur* [that] was
displeasing to the lady's parents," and through whose "agency
the young poet lover was banished from the court."[7] This story
of love and sentiment was not unfamiliar to Dickinson, who
was already well-versed in Elizabeth Barrett's poetry, including, it can be assumed, her tributes to Camões in poems such
as "A Vision of Poets," "Lady Geraldine's Courtship," and, above
all, "Catarina to Camoëns."

If Higginson did not take much direct action on behalf of
what he saw as Camões's dwindling English-language reputation, he did offer his gesture. By translating two of the Portuguese poet's sonnets, he acknowledged his importance to the
sonnet tradition emanating from Petrarch. Higginson's love for
the sonnet form led him to champion the sonnet in English. In
the preface to the edition of *American Sonnets* that he and E.H.
Bigelow published in 1890, he takes issue with Coleridge's rather
harsh remarks regarding the inevitably prosy productions that
resulted from the misguided attempts of the moderns to recre-
ate in English the largely Petrarchan sonnet.[8] That disagreement with the great Romantic poet did not keep Higginson from
paying his own tribute to the sources of the European sonnet
by translating Petrarch as well as Camões. Examples of those
translations appear in *The Afternoon Landscape: Poems and
Translations*, published in 1889; in 1903 he collected his Petrarch
translations in *Fifteen Sonnets of Petrarch*, which appeared in a
small deluxe edition with the Italian and English on facing
pages.[9]

The first of Higginson's two translations of Camões's son-nets is a version of "Lindo e subtil trançăo, que ficaste." In *Af-ternoon Landscape* it is preceded by the following statement acknowledging the provenance of his own interest in Camões: "Mrs. Browning in 'Catarina to Camoens' represents her as be-queathing him the ribbon from her hair; but she in reality gave it to him during her life as a substitute for the ringlet for which he pleaded."

> O ribbon fair, that dost with me remain
>   In pawn for that sweet gift I do deserve,
>   If but to win thee makes my reason swerve,
>   What were it if one ringlet I could gain?
> Those golden locks thy circling knots restrain,
>   Locks whose bright rays might well for sunbeams serve,
>   When thou unloosest each fair coil and curve,
>   Oh is it to beguile, or slay with pain?
> Dear ribbon, in my hand I hold thee now;
>   And were it only to assuage my grief,
>   Since I can have thee only, cling to thee,
> Yet tell her, thou canst never fill my vow,
>   But in the reckoning of love's fond belief
>   This gift for that whole debt a pledge shall be.[10]

The second sonnet, a version of "Os olhos onde o casto Amor ardia," is preceded by a quotation of two lines from Elizabeth Barrett Browning's poem, "Lady Geraldine's Courtship": "For we had been reading Camoens,—that poem, you remember, / Which his lady's eyes were praised in, as the sweetest ever seen." ("I hope I have not tired 'Sweetest Eyes were ever seen,'" wrote Emily Dickinson to a friend.)[11] Higginson probably first encoun-tered the poem "Lady Geraldine's Courtship" in his early twen-ties, it has been suggested, just at the time that "Barbara Channing brought from Brook Farm a manuscript copy of two new poems by a young Englishwoman named Elizabeth Barrett." One of those poems was called "Lay of the Brown Rosary," the other "Lady Geraldine's Courtship." All "the Brook Farm literati were mad about them," writes Anna Mary Wells, "and learning them by heart."[12] Here is Higginson's translation of Camões's sonnet:

Those eyes from whence chaste love was wont to glow,
    And smiled to see his torches kindled there;
    That face within whose beauty strange and rare
            The rosy light of dawn gleamed o'er the snow;
That hair, which bid the envious sun to know
    His brightest beams less golden rays did wear;
    That pure white hand, the gracious form and fair:
    All these into the dust of earth must go.
O perfect beauty in its tenderest age!
    O flower cut down ere it could all unfold
    By the stern hand of unrelenting death!
Why did not Love itself quit earth's poor stage,
    Not because here dwelt beauty's perfect mould,
    But that so soon it passed from mortal breath?[13]

Higginson, too—like his self-proclaimed student from
Amherst—focused on Camões's attraction to the eyes of lovers.
And like Higginson, Emily Dickinson knew well Elizabeth
Browning's *Sonnets from the Portuguese*, too.

Dickinson valued Elizabeth Browning. In her second letter
to Higginson she listed her as one of the three poets she read
(the others being John Keats and Robert Browning) and she
displayed one of the three pictures she owned of the author of
Aurora Leigh in her bedroom. She did not, however, value the
Sonnets more highly than did Higginson. For he found no Portuguese poetry, beyond that of Camões—not that of Gil Vicente,
Saa de Miranda, Antonio Ferreira, or Violante do Ceo—"com-
parable to Elizabeth Barrett's imaginary sonnets from the Portuguese."[14] It is no surprise that Dickinson offered him one of
her three pictures of Browning.

As for the relationship that those sonnets seemed to document, as late as 1900, in *Women and the Alphabet*, Higginson
could celebrate: "What a step from the horrible nuptials of those
savage days to the poetic marriage of Robert Browning and
Elizabeth Barrett—the 'Sonnets from the Portuguese' on one
side, the 'One Word More' on the other!" Then, thinking ahead,
he writes presciently: "But who can say that the whole relation
between man and woman reached its climax there, and that
where the past has brought changes so vast the future is to add

nothing? Who knows that, when 'the world's great bridals come,' people may not look back with pity, even on this era of the Brownings? Perhaps even Elizabeth Barrett promised to obey!"[15] To his credit, Higginson had not fixed unremittingly on Elizabeth Barrett's own decision to choose the Camonean virtues of courtly love and obeisance.

It is doubtful that Emily Dickinson knew Camões's poetry directly, that is to say, either the Portuguese (or Spanish) originals, though she might have known Camões in translation. She did know about Camões through her reading of *The Indicator* and, perhaps, Longfellow. But it was Elizabeth Barrett Browning's poetry that most moved her. As we have seen, she echoed the refrain from "Catarina to Camoëns" in her letters.[16] To Mrs. Holland she wrote, "for Katrina's Eyes, Camoens is sorry."[17] Here the code is simple. Emily (like Camões) reacts to Katrina's eyes, which in this case show the signs of worry and, undoubtedly, weeping. This Katrina is Mrs. Holland's daughter Kate, who has been troubled recently by her husband's illness.[18] In an earlier letter, it was Mrs. Holland herself whom Dickinson cast as Catarina, as she apologized: "I hope I have not tired 'Sweetest Eyes were ever seen,' for whose beloved Acts, both revealed and covert, I am each Day more fondly, their Possessor's Own."[19] It seems obvious that in Elizabeth Barrett Browning's poem on Catarina de Ataide these two friends found meaning that they could adapt to their own relationship.

If Dickinson knew "Catarina to Camoëns" well enough to quote from it, she probably also knew the two other Browning poems that mention Camões, "A Vision of Poets" and "Lady Geraldine's Courtship." In "A Vision of Poets" she writes of the Camões who was the author of the epic poem *Os Lusíadas*:

> And Camoens, with that look he had,
> Compelling India's Genius sad
> From the wave through the Lusiad . . .[20]

In "Lady Geraldine's Courtship," the earlier of the two poems, she writes of Camões, the author of sonnets and madrigals:

And this morning, as I sat alone within the inner chamber
With the great saloon beyond it, lost in pleasant thought
    serene—
For I had been reading Camoëns—that poem you remember,
Which his lady's eyes are praised in, as the sweetest ever
    seen.[21]

Doubtless much of Dickinson's knowledge of the love between Camões and Catarina de Ataide came from her reading
of Elizabeth Barrett Browning's poems, especially "Catarina to
Camoëns." But a good deal of information about Camões was
available in Longfellow's introductory matter in *Poets and Poetry of Europe* as well as, as has been suggested, in the first issue of *The Indicator* in 1848.

That Browning's poem was particularly memorable to
Dickinson we know from her use of phrases and images from
the poem in letters to her friend, Mrs. J.G. Holland. But it can
be speculated that the matter of the poem might have had a
closer personal meaning for Miss Dickinson of Amherst, if she
was separated, as has been suggested—by a few miles or by the
breadth of a continent—from the person (or persons) she felt
most strongly and most sentimentally about. Given such sepa-
rations, her situation seemed to replicate that of Catarina in
Lisbon while Camões was off in Africa. The poet could consider the death of the young Catarina, unbeknownst to her lover,
who was in distant exile. Elizabeth Browning's poetic creation
of the dying Catarina's final words to her absent poet-lover typi-
fied the sort of literary production that attracted the sentimental reader of the day.

Dickinson knew, of course, the basic story of the star-crossed
lovers—what has been called the "central story of nineteenth-
century literature, of the marriage made in heaven, prevented
on earth, but to be celebrated eternally in heaven"—particularly as they were told by the Brontës in *Jane Eyre* and *Wuthering
Heights*.[22] Along with Elizabeth Barrett Browning, she might
also have known *Letters of a Portuguese Nun*. First published in
French in 1669 as *Lettres d'une religieuse portugaise* and translated into English by 1678, these are the love letters of a young

religious addressed to the French military officer who has se-
duced and abandoned her. Remarks in the introduction to one
of the nineteenth-century English-language editions of *Letters*
(published in 1890, coincidentally the year which saw the publication of the first volume of Dickinson poems) seem particularly appropriate to a consideration of the Amherst poet who,
choosing privacy, affected white for her everyday dress.

> The figure of the Portuguese nun glides among the shadows,
> and other shadows arise—a vision of white-robed and black-
> robed sisters, the veiled forms of nuns silently winding along,—
> Heloise is there, for whom heaven itself holds only Abelard—the
> sainted Theresa with breast pierced by the flame-tipped arrow,
> symbol of the divine love which has entered her soul—the lovely
> Louise de la Vallière, the petted favorite of a court, doing pen-
> ance in solitude and tears for having loved too much,—and how
> vast a throng besides of ardent and gracious beings, brides of
> heaven or earth, all alike kindled with the passion, whether
> mystic or human, which radiates from the inner Life and Light,
> breathing through the world.[23]

I would broach fleetingly one other matter regarding Emily
Dickinson's possible knowledge of *Letters of a Portuguese Nun*.
Mariana Alcoforado's series of letters offers one model for the
so-called "Master" letters found among Dickinson's manuscripts
and never really explained satisfactorily. They seem to share
the essential aspects of the lover-letter motif: "engagement,
absences of the love partner, and imaginative, linguistic com-
pensation through letter-writing."[24] If Dickinson's fragments—
whether authentic letters or fictional ones ("those surcharged
and passionate epistles expressing a love that was not returned,"
writes Richard B. Sewall, Dickinson's biographer[25])—were intended to form a sequence, Dickinson could have found no
model more *à propos* to her purposes than *Letters of a Portuguese Nun*, that collection, as the official privileging note of the
French in 1668 put it, "Les Valentines lettres."[26] It may be mere
coincidence, but a so-called "valentine letter" by Dickinson was
published in the Amherst College literary journal *The Indicator*
in 1850.[27]

8

Elizabeth Bishop's Black Gold

In the early 1950s Elizabeth Bishop reviewed two books on Emily Dickinson, both for the *New Republic*. Her review of *Emily Dickinson's Letters to Doctor and Mrs. Josiah Gilbert Holland* appeared in August 1951, and her review of *The Riddle of Emily Dickinson* a year later.[1] Bishop liked Theodora Van Wagenen Ward's "beautifully edited" volume of the poet's letters to the Hollands. She did not like Rebecca Patterson's book of "literary detective-work," though the book dealt with lesbianism, a subject that was very much on Bishop's mind at the time, according to her biographer.[2] In Dickinson's letters to the Hollands she probably read past those gnomic references to Elizabeth Barrett's poem "Catarina to Camoëns" that would have meant more to her a few months later, when, unexpectedly, she settled in Brazil for an indefinite stay that would last nearly two decades.

In late 1951 Bishop set out on a voyage intended to take her, eventually, around the world. On 10 November, in New York, she boarded a freighter bound for Tierra del Fuego and the Straits of Magellan. Two days out to sea, her mind was on her unfinished review of *The Riddle of Emily Dickinson*, as she revealed to a friend:

> I am reviewing that god awful Emily Dickinson book by a Mrs Patterson for the New R.—although Johnson in the Times Sunday before last did such an excellent job nothing more remains to be said. May said some thing funny, though, and I'm going to use it—giving her some sort of credit:
>
> > Kate Scott!
> > Great Scott![3]

Bishop's review did not appear until 18 August 1952—a delay that prompted her to note on her typescript copy of the review that because there had been a change in editors at the *New Republic* the review had never appeared. Her typescript shows that she ended her review:

> Or, as a poetic friend of mine better summarized it:
>
> Kate Scott!
> Great Scott![4]

The new editor, apparently without authorization from Bishop, dropped this final sentence quoting the poet May Swenson.

Bishop was unsympathetic to *The Riddle of Emily Dickinson*, Rebecca Patterson's "literary detective-work" that led to the identification of Mrs. Kate Anthon (*née* Scott) as the object of the New England poet's "hopeless passion." Bishop did not deny entirely Patterson's thesis: "the two young women met and fell in love; about a year later Kate Scott broke it off in some way, and Emily Dickinson had been christened and launched on her life of increasing sorrow and seclusion. . . . That her thesis is partially true might have occurred to any reader of Emily Dickinson's poetry—occurred on one page to be contradicted on the next."

Bishop's travel plans in 1951 included a short layover in Rio de Janeiro. In late November, she left the SS *Bowplate* at Santos, and by 30 November she was in Rio de Janeiro. Later she would imply that she had arrived at that seaport, an hour's drive from São Paulo, in "January 1952," the date she assigned her poem "Arrival at Santos" when it appeared in the *New Yorker* on 21 June 1952. When the poem was first published in book form, as the penultimate poem in *Poems: North & South—A Cold Spring* (1955), Bishop dropped the date, only to restore it in *Questions of Travel* (1965). That restoration, speculates David Kalstone, helps to link "Arrival at Santos," placed first in *Questions of Travel* (1965), to the book's second poem, "Brazil, January 1, 1502."

That Bishop fell seriously ill during her stay in Rio, and that in the course of her convalescence she fell in love with her friend Lota de Macedo Soares, is a familiar tale to Bishop's readers.

The result for Bishop of these entwined occurrences was that she would henceforth make her home with Lota in Brazil, a decision that opened up for her the opportunity to turn her intelligence and sensibility toward a new relationship, a new country, and a new continent. Even before falling ill, Bishop had begun to write "Arrival at Santos," and it would be the first of her Brazil poems to be finished and, in 1952, published. The second poem in the "Brazil" section of *Questions of Travel* was not finished until shortly before New Year's Day 1959. To mark the date for Robert Lowell she sent him "Brazil, January 1, 1502." "Jungle into picture into history and then jungle again," Lowell characterized it.[5]

For "Brazil, January 1, 1502" Bishop has chosen an epigraph: "embroidered nature . . . tapestried landscape," which she attributes to Sir Kenneth Clark (*Landscape into Art*). Since the poem takes as its subject the arrival of the first Portuguese at the place they misnamed Rio de Janeiro, thinking it was a river, Bishop might as readily have quoted from Camões's Canto IX of *Os Lusíadas* those lines devoted to the imaginary "Island of Love."[6] "Unknown to geography," as the future author of *Geography III* might have read in C.M. Bowra's well-known book on the epic,[7] this timeless place is described, in William Julius Mickle's translation:

> Far o'er the shadowy vale their carpets spread,
> Of fairer *tapestry*, and of richer bloom,
> Than ever glow'd in Persia's boasted loom:
> As glittering rainbows o'er the verdure thrown,
> O'er every woodland walk th' *embroidery* shone.[8]

But Camões's suitability to Bishop's poem goes beyond the echo of a word or two in the phrases she has chosen for her epigraph. It will be recalled that the vision of the fabled "Island of Love" and what will happen there are the rewards Venus bestows on the successful Portuguese mariners. In an episode of free and boundless sex, Vasco da Gama's sailors mate with nymphs in a luxuriously pastoral setting.

> Through the rough Brakes and Woods darted they All.
> The Nymphs went flying the thick boughs between,

Yet not so Swift as Artificial.
  Shreeking, and laughing softly in the close,
  They let the Greyhounds gain upon the Does.[9]

In Bishop's poem the Portuguese mariners "came and found it all, / not unfamiliar." Although they found "no lovers' walks, no bowers, / no cherries to be picked, not lute music," what they found was familiar to them, "corresponding, nevertheless, / to an old dream of wealth and luxury / already out of style when they left home—/ wealth, plus a brand-new pleasure." Their old dream of riches and luxury (in a Dickinsonian sense—see her "Wild Nights—Wild Nights! / Were I with thee / Wild Nights should be / Our luxury!") would have had its literary source for the Portuguese in Camões's account of Gama's sailors sporting on the "Island of Love." But history does not mesh readily with imagination, not even that romance incorporated into an historical epic. At least not the history imagined in "Brazil, January 1, 1502," which records that the sailors "ripped away into the hanging fabric,"

> each out to catch an Indian for himself—
> those maddening little women who kept calling
> each to each other (or had the birds waked up?)
> and retreating, always retreating, behind it.

Always retreating in the sylvan scene—here Bishop pays homage to Keats's "Ode on a Grecian Urn." One must *assume* that outside of the "tapestry" of Bishop's poem, rapes took place. What the poem does not allow for (recall that "always") is that the Indian nymphs acquiesced in the way Camões's "Does" (being "not so Swift as Artificial") allowed the pursuing "Greyhounds" to gain on them. The Indian women in Bishop's poem—if not in history or in the romantic fantasy of Camões's "Island of Love"—remain forever unravished like the nymphs on the frieze of the urn considered in Keats's famous poem.

If in recent years scholars have cast doubt over the authenticity of Camões's authorship of the sonnet beginning "Quem vê, Senhora, claro e manifesto," there was no such doubt in Bishop's time.[10] It appears in such popular collections of Camões's po-

etry as Rodrigues Lapa's selection of *Líricas* (in a fifth edition
by 1970) and in the small-sized Edições de Ouro volume available throughout Brazil in the 1960s. In *Questions of Travel*
Bishop quotes from Camões's poem. The poem can be rendered
into English:

> If one, my Lady, seeing clearly and manifestly
> the fineness of your beautiful eyes,
> is not blinded by the very sight of them,
> that one has not paid you what is your due.
> Such seems fair enough price to me; but I,
> having the advantage of deserving them, gave
> over even more, my life and soul, for wanting
> them, leaving me nothing else besides.
> Thus my life, my soul, my hope, all
> that I have—all of it is yours—
> and the profit taken is mine alone.
> Because it brings me such great bliss
> giving you what I have and what I may,
>   the more I give you, the more I owe you.
>
> (Quem vê, Senhora, claro e manifesto
> o lindo ser de vossos olhos belos,
> se não perder a vista só em vê-los,
> já não paga o que deve a vosso gesto.
> Este me parecia preço honesto;
> mas eu, por de vantagem merecê-los,
> dei mais a vida e alma por querê-los,
> donde já me não fica mais de resto.
> Assi que a vida e alma e esperança
> e tudo quanto tenho, tudo é vosso,
> e o proveito disso eu só o levo.
> Porque é tamanha bem-aventurança
> o dar-vos quanto tenho e quanto posso,
> que, quanto mais vos pago, mais vos devo.)[11]

From this sonnet Elizabeth Bishop took over the last two
lines as part of her dedication of *Questions of Travel* to Lota,
her Brazilian lover.

> . . . *O dar-vos quanto tenho e quanto posso,*
> *Que quanto mais vos pago, mais vos devo.*[12]

(Giving you what I have and what I may,
The more I give you, the more I owe you.)

As amply shown in her work with modern Brazilian poets and
her rendering of *Minha Vida de Menina* (published as *The Diary
of "Helena Morley"*), Bishop became adept at translating from
the Portuguese, but in this instance she chose to invoke Camões
only in the original.[13] "The dedication is very simple," she explained to American friends, "it is such a well-known quotation in Portugese [*sic*] that it doesn't sound quite as corny in
Portugese as it will to you, maybe, when you get it translated."[14]
Most of Bishop's critics seem not to have tried to work out the
English meaning of Camões's lines or to have looked into the
poem from which Bishop had taken them. In fact, only one reviewer of *Questions of Travel* even mentions the lines from
Camões, but that one mention is suggestive. Frank Warnke sees
them as linking Bishop to "that earlier poet-traveler" who also
"finds in the act of travel an expression of those impossible and
deeply human . . ." (quoting from "Arrival at Santos")

> . . . demands for a different world,
> and a better life, and complete comprehension
> of both at last, and immediately . . .[15]

Camões as traveler (albeit sometimes a reluctant one) certainly
"fits" him to the title of Bishop's book, supporting one of its
major themes. That the lines are attributable to Camões estab-
lishes this connection, though Warnke's insight might have resulted from his having known the poet when the two of them
were at the University of Washington. "He was a professor at
the Un. of Washington. Did this as a SURPRISE for me—very
nice of him," Bishop scrawled across the top margin of her copy
of Warnke's review.[16] That the lines quoted from Camões are
those of a poet-lover no reviewer, not even Warnke, even hints
at. But that fact is Bishop's major reason for appropriating them.
Moreover, if the two lines quoted were not enough to indicate
it, the Camonean sonnet from which they are derived goes a
long way, in its entirety, toward establishing *Questions of Travel*
as a lover's book, one in which the poet performs for her lover,
much as jugglers in the Middle Ages performed for the Blessed

Virgin, first on Brazilian themes and then on "elsewhere" (largely "northern") themes. The point of Bishop's dedication may be missed if one insists too strenuously that "her published work on the erotic or intimate relationships of her life stopped in *A Cold Spring*."[17] Of course, her decision to print Camões's lines in the original Portuguese might suggest evasion.

It is not unlikely that Camões's sonnet held private meanings for the two of them—Elizabeth and Lota—though such meanings are not evident. In adopting Camões's words, Bishop leaves us evidence of the intensity of her attachment to Lota, that woman—in Elizabeth Hardwick's words—"very intense indeed, emotional, also a bit insecure as we say, and loyal, devoted and smart and lesbian and Brazilian and shy, masterful in some ways, but helpless also," who for fifteen years enabled Bishop to have a Brazilian life.[18]

On the dust jacket (back) of *Questions of Travel*, which Bishop thought "rather pretty . . . bit too chi-chi possibly," appears a reproduction of a drawing of Bishop by the Brazilian artist Darcy Penteado.[19] "I don't think much of that drawing, really," she confessed, "but you know how they insist on photography—and I refused and refused and then it was a choice between this drawing and a lot of blurbs—so I decided this was a bit more impersonal and would also please my Brazilian friends."[20] This disclaimer aside, she liked it well enough to release it to Brazilian newspapers well in advance of the book's publication to be used along with "Dia de Reis," a Portuguese translation of her poem "Twelfth Morning; or What You Will."

Darcy Penteado, as Bishop identified him, was "a very young man who did a lot of society portraits, etc., here a few years ago—now I hear he is doing pop art in Rome!"[21] But Darcy had one other minor accomplishment that might have brought him to Bishop's attention. In 1956 he had illustrated the first collection of Emily Dickinson's poems published in Brazil.[22] That he was thus linked to Dickinson leads to a thought. Bishop said she admired the Amherst poet for "having dared to do it, all alone."[23] Yet she also disapproved of Dickinson's "narrowing of poetic subject to 'love, human and divine,'" a complaint that has led one critic to speculation—"to think that Bishop may

have considered a part of her own twentieth-century emanci-
pation from stereotypic womanhood to have been release from
that entrapping woman's subject, love."[24] But the release from
that "woman's subject," if there was a release, was not apparent in 1965, when Bishop published some of her most closely
thought-out Brazilian poems in the book she not merely dedicated to her Brazilian lover but so designed as to make a private point.

   Questions of Travel contains nineteen poems and one story.
The first eleven poems are in a section called "Brazil," and the
story and the eight poems that follow it are in a section called
"Elsewhere." The Brazilian poems include some of her most
admired work—"Arrival at Santos," "Brazil, January 1, 1502,"
"Questions of Travel," "Manuelzinho," "The Armadillo," "The
Riverman," "Twelfth Morning; or What You Will," and "The
Burglar of Babylon." The work in the "Elsewhere" section of
the book has as its predominant setting the Canadian Maritimes.
These include a short story (a longish one, for Bishop) about
Nova Scotia, and at least three poems identifiably Nova Scotian.
These two halves of the book—"Brazil" and "Elsewhere"—stand
for the poles around which Bishop organizes her experience as
of 1965—the two hemispheres, north and south (recalling the
title of her first volume of poems, published in 1946, six years
before she arrived in Brazil—when the poles of her experience
were Nova Scotia in the north and Key West in the south). Read
from first page to last, *Questions of Travel* can be seen as a statement of where the poet stood at the time, where she had been,
and the different place from which, it can be said, she had come.
From this point of view, *Questions of Travel* can be seen as a
showing forth of her poet's wares and her love for the person to
whom she has dedicated her book of poems. Read as a book
made public, to be sure, but openly dedicated to Lota, *Questions of Travel* becomes one more of the singular gifts given to
illustrate and reaffirm the personal truth of the lines she quotes
from Camões: "Giving you what I have and what I may, / The
more I give you, the more I owe you."

   Questions of Travel was published on 29 November 1965. We
now know that by then Bishop was already feeling strong pres-

sures and burdensome demands stemming in large part from
Lota's own exhaustion and deteriorating health. We also know
that, possibly in reaction to such changes in Lota, Bishop was
turning toward at least one "other"—to be named later. With
the benefit of hindsight, the attentive reader will realize that
the epigraph from Camões can be looked at in a second, more
skeptical, way. Besides the possibility of its being read as a direct expression of love, it might also be read as a lover's complaint—that giving one's all is not only not requital enough but
that in giving all one actually increases, paradoxically, the remaining debt. Already manifest in 1965 were the signs of the
disintegration of Bishop's and Lota's relationship—anger, ac-
cusations, unkindness, an affair, even Bishop's quietly defiant
assertion of independence in purchasing a seemingly unneeded
house in Ouro Prêto. The almost total disintegration of the
Bishop-Lota relationship was imminent, coming to a head at
the end of 1966. By the first of the year, Bishop "had packed a
suitcase and had moved out of the apartment and into a Rio
hotel. . . . Out 'in half an hour,'" she complained, "'after fifteen
years with a few dirty clothes in a busted suitcase, no home
any more, no claim (legally) to anything here.'"[25]

It will surprise no one that these contra-temps in a sentimental tragedy should have worked their way into the poet's
poetry. But just how Bishop used her poetry in her quotidian
life is not without its curious and strange interest. That Bishop's
two-part scheme for the arrangement of her poems in *Questions of Travel*—"Brazil" and "Elsewhere"—was not merely a per-
functory act of arrangement but might well have carried private
messages for Lota gains support from a Bishop love poem only
recently discovered.

Among the pleasures in Lloyd Schwartz's 1991 *New Yorker*
piece is a "new" poem to be added to the clutch of poems Bishop
wrote during her Brazilian life.[26] This untitled work—twenty-
four lines broken down into six four-line stanzas—is indisput-
ably a highly personal love poem, but it is atypically so in that
it treats erotic content directly. It is a poem of intervention; that
is to say, its intent, chiding lightly as it does, is to persuade. As
such, it may have been "too personal to make public," as
Schwartz speculates, or "even keep a copy of" for herself.

Dear, my compass
still points north
to wooden houses
and blue eyes,

fairy-tales where
flaxen-headed
younger sons
bring home the goose,

love in hay-lofts,
Protestants, and
heavy drinkers . . .
Springs are backward,

but crab-apples
ripen to rubies,
cranberries
to drops of blood,

and swans can paddle
icy water,
so hot the blood
in those webbed feet.

—Cold as it is, we'd
go to bed, dear,
early, but never
to keep warm.[27]

Schwartz tells us that he learned of this poem in 1990 while visiting Ouro Prêto, the small colonial town in the state of Minas Gerais where Bishop had purchased the house she named Vila Mariana (in part, for Marianne Moore). The poem was shown to him by Lilli Correia de Araújo, the owner of the Pouso do Chico Rey, a small inn in Ouro Prêto, and Lota's friend as well as (briefly—probably as early as 1965) one of Bishop's lovers. ("Elizabeth always had to be in love and she fell in love easily," Lilli said later, but "she also fell out of love easily."[28]) That affair is perhaps obliquely reflected in the poem Bishop dedicated to Lilli, "Under the Window: Ouro Preto."[29] Millier, Bishop's biographer, seems to imply that it was the appearance of this poem in the 24 December 1966 issue of the *New Yorker* that brought about what turned out to be the irreparable rupture between Lota and Elizabeth.[30]

The "new" poem transcribed from the copy in the possession of Lilli Correia de Araújo is part of the story of that break. Its tone is explanatory, with a hint of apology. It is directed to someone identified only as "dear" (a term that, depending on a context the poem does not give us, can hint at either closeness or distance). That the intended auditor of the poem is native to the Southern hemisphere seems to be indicated by the nature of the speaker's explanation: her compass points "north" where "Springs are backward." Millier reproduces this untitled poem, preceding it with an informative paragraph:

> Lilli kept her husband's beautiful paintings of women hanging all around her house and inn. Since his death in 1955, she had had only lesbian relationships, thereby preserving his memory, she said. Lilli herself was tall, blond, and Nordic looking, and the two women [Lilli and Elizabeth] shared an occasional nostalgia for northern things, especially the spring. Among the objects Elizabeth left for Lilli was a poem, framed in her own watercolor illustrations, that speaks to that common nostalgia; the different, yet reminiscent, chill of the mountain air; and the painful compromises their love involved; and the sheer joy of their intimacy.[31]

Undoubtedly Bishop and Lilli shared a nostalgia for things "northern," but it does not seem to me that this poem is addressed to Lilli. It is more plausible that it is addressed to Lota, as originally intended. If this is so, as I think it is, Bishop's leaving the poem with the (temporary) lover who was originally Lota's friend, suggests something about the nature of Bishop's changing relationship with Lota and Lilli. With the gift of this poem Bishop extended the secret meaning of what Ouro Prêto had come to mean to her. Intended, perhaps, as an intervention to be used directly with a primary lover, the poem is presented to a second lover undoubtedly possessing intimate knowledge of the poet's primary relationship.

What one might now call the Lota—Lilli—Elizabeth poem warrants, therefore, a closer, more formal look. In his *New*

Yorker piece Schwartz points to touches that are characteristically Bishop's: "the fairy-tale vividness and coloring-book clarity of her images . . .; the geographical references—and restlessness—of the world traveller; the delicate yet sharply etched jokes, often at her own expense ('Protestants, and / heavy drinkers': she was both); the apparent conversational casualness disguising the formality of the versification; the understated yet urgent sexuality; even the identification with animals."

It is notable that Schwartz was shown not one manuscript but two: one handwritten, the other typed—both of them "illuminated in the roomy margins with small watercolors by Bishop: a square brown house, an apple tree, a goose, a hayloft with a pitchfork, a swan with its head disappearing in the text of the poem, and a fourposter bed." Yet Bishop not only did not publish the poem, she virtually "abandoned it in Brazil," writes Schwartz, "with typical obliqueness, it is even *about* Brazil—or, rather, what Brazil is not. She must have been living there for more than a decade when she wrote it, probably in the mid-nineteen-sixties, and of the poems she wrote there it is the only one—at least, the only one that has come to light—in which she weighs the world of her childhood in Nova Scotia against the life she chose for herself later, in which she measures not only how far she has travelled from her origins but how difficult it is to escape them."

It is possible to see the matter differently. True, Bishop never published the poem and apparently kept no copy of it for herself. And true, Bishop did finally leave Brazil to live out her last years in New England. But the poem does not deal with such matters. It offers an implied comparison of the poet's earlier formative life in the cold north with her "dear's" warmer south, and it does so for a purpose. The poem strikes the reader as being very private, one not intended for auction or re-collection in a book. Its tone is suasive, its intention seduction. It is meant, perhaps, to have its effect, specifically, on one person. Given to that person in handwritten form, it could do the specific work the poet wished it to do. It is not irrelevant that although both the holograph manuscript and the typed version are illustrated apparently with the "same" drawings, as Schwartz tells us, "the images on the typed copy appeared in a different order, but incised pencil outlines suggest that they may have been traced from the handwritten original." Rather than abandoning the poem or even merely leaving it behind when she left Brazil for the last time, Bishop gave away not just copies of the poem, but the ontological poem itself. Her act in this instance recalls, incidentally, those many instances when Emily Dickinson "gave" away a poem, incorporating it into a homespun emblem or weaving it into the text of a familiar letter.

Just how deeply "Portuguese" Bishop had become by the time she composed this lover's poem emerges in a simple detail, a touch no Portuguese reader would need to make a point of. Bishop knew Brazilian culture and the country's language well enough to build her poem around a single Portuguese word that, given the object of her poem as a personal communication to one specific listener, is omitted from the poem. The word is *nortear*. A verb, which in the infinitive, is literally rendered as "to north," *nortear* means "to guide, direct or lead one's self." Bishop's play on this ultimately nautical word, indicating not merely her bio-geographical origins but her continuing sources of orientation, would seem entirely natural to a Brazilian (or Portuguese) reader. One imagines that the poet, not truly apologizing for her "northern" origin (or, therefore, "northern" orientation), offers her explanations that it is their exposure to northern cold that enables "crab-apples [to] ripen to rubies" and "cranberries" to turn into "drops of blood," as fortifying facts for her chiding revelation to her southern "dear" that up there, human beings "go to bed . . . / early, but never / to keep warm."

Unlike Bishop's other poems, this newly discovered poem was intended to share its subject *not* with the person who now reads it but with the one person who would understand the one "other" about whom it was written. It was in Brazil that this "new" poem meant most—as the poet intended.[32] Yet it also casts light on the secret only hinted at in the Portuguese of Luis de Camões that graces the dedication page of *Questions of Travel*.

This poem, unlike the relationship to which it now testifies, turns out to be something other than still another thing filled with the intent to be lost—like the lost door keys, the hour badly spent, and the three loved houses that went ("One Art").[33] The

late poem "One Art" is both a testament to certain feelings of
elegy and loss and a poem intended—in conception, revision,
and publication—as an intervention in her own life. (That the
poem continued to have its effect on the poet is apparent in
her self-accusation, after she had lost a writing case containing much of her unfinished work, "Oh why did I write that
cursed villanelle?"[34]) In this poem about the self's attempt to
survive a new or impending loss, Bishop refers, too, to Lota; in
a strange way, Camões, too, has a ghostly presence in the
poem.[35] Lota has become still one more loss—the greatest, perhaps, of such losses—in the litany of loss the poet sets down in
a poem published nine years after Lota's death in 1967.

> The art of losing isn't hard to master;
> so many things seem filled with the intent
> to be lost that their loss is no disaster.
>
> Lose something every day. Accept the fluster
> of lost door keys, the hour badly spent.
> The art of losing isn't hard to master.
>
> Then practice losing farther, losing faster;
> places, and names, and where it was you meant
> to travel. None of these will bring disaster.
>
> I lost my mother's watch. And look! my last, or
> next-to-last, of three loved houses went.
> The art of losing isn't hard to master.
>
> I lost two cities, lovely ones. And, vaster,
> some realms I owned, two rivers, a continent.
> I miss them, but it wasn't a disaster.
>
> —Even losing you (the joking voice, a gesture
> I love) I shan't have lied. It's evident
> the art of losing's not too hard to master
> though it may look like (*Write* it!) like disaster.[36]

The poem's key—linguistic, lexical, phonic—is obviously the
rhyming words "master" and "disaster." That the poem is a
villanelle enables this rhyme to occur seven times. Indeed, "The

repetitions of the key rhyme words, *master* and *disaster*," writes the critic Lorrie Goldensohn, "alternate in the obsessive and tragic dilemma of the grief-stricken speaker, as like a too-tightly wound spring the poem breaks to its conclusion, the painful subversion of language and form by feeling."[37] This rhyme did not appear until the second (extant) draft of "One Art."[38]

Now it is of course possible that Bishop hit on the "master-disaster" rhyme on her own, but it is worth considering the possibility that it is derivative. The possibilities are suggestive. One of them occurs in one of the half-dozen or so most famous poems in the English language. Edgar Allan Poe employs the "master-disaster" rhyme in "The Raven," that great poem of irrevocable loss:

> "Doubtless," said I, "what it utters is its only stock and store
> Caught from some unhappy master whom unmerciful Disaster
> Followed fast and followed faster till his songs one burden bore—
> Till the dirges of his Hope that melancholy burden bore
>   Of 'Never—nevermore.'"[39]

Poe not only anticipates Bishop's "master-disaster" rhyme but, remarkably, her triple rhyme as well: "master-disaster-faster":

> The art of losing isn't hard to master.
>
> Then practice losing farther, losing faster;
> places, and names, and where it was you meant
> to travel. None of these will bring disaster.

A second possible source for Bishop's "master-disaster" rhyme is a poem by the Southern African poet Roy Campbell. His sonnet entitled "Luis de Camões" celebrates the Portuguese poet's ability to make poetry out of adversity ("fire and shipwreck, pestilence and loss"). The rhyming of "disaster" and "master" occurs in the first quatrain:

> Camões, alone of all the lyric race,
> Born in the angry morning of disaster
> Can look a common soldier in the face.
> I find a comrade where I sought a master

For daily, while the stinking crocodiles
Glide from the mangroves on the swampy shore,
He shares my awning on the dhow, he smiles
And tells me that he lived it all before.
Through fire and shipwreck, pestilence and loss,
Led by the *ignis fatuus* of duty
To a dog's death—yet of his sorrows king—
He shouldered high his voluntary Cross,
Wrestled his hardships into forms of beauty,
And taught his gorgon destinies to sing.[40]

As Campbell notes, Camões had "lived it all before" ("fire and shipwreck, pestilence and loss"). Indeed, as Bishop undoubtedly knows, it was something more than just the romantic's take on his life that Camões had suffered through the disasters of losing "houses," lovers, and even his work.

It is possible that when in "One Art" Bishop worked her magical craft—her "mechanical devising of rhymes"[41]—she did not consciously recall that her poem might be indebted to either Poe or Campbell. But whether or not she was so influenced, there is no gainsaying that she makes the rhyme her own, bringing about its large effect by rhyming "master" with "disaster," over and over again—or, as she said, "This is a villanelle—it repeats & repeats & *repeats*."[42] Marianne Moore had Bishop in mind when she reminded that "an indebted thing does not interest us unless there is originality underneath it."[43] It may be that Bishop's settling on the villanelle—this "rare excursion . . . into a complex, pre-existent verse pattern," notes Schwartz—enabled her to focus clearly on the essential elements of her material.[44]

It has been said that in "One Art" Bishop "confronts the death of Lota de Macedo Soares with understated but searing directness."[45] Bishop did not think so, apparently, for to the end of her life she planned to write a book-length poem to commemorate Lota. "Only the barest outline of 'Elegy' is left among Elizabeth's papers," according to her biographer.

It indicates that she planned to write the poem "in sections, some anecdotal, some lyrical, different [lengths] – never more than two short pages–." The poem was to be an elegy for Lota

Soares; her "reticence and pride"; her "heroism, brave &
young"; her "beautiful colored skin"; "the gestures (which [you]
said you didn't have)." The poem was also to investigate specific memories: "the [door] slamming, plaster-falling –the [cook]
and I laughing helplessly"; Lota's "courage to the last, or almost to the last–"; "regret and guilt, the nighttime horrors";
"WASTE."[46]

It was not to be. As it turned out, her last poem would be about
herself. Three weeks after her death on 6 October 1979, the *New
Yorker* published her "Sonnet":

> Caught—the bubble
> in the spirit-level,
> a creature divided;
> and the compass needle
> wobbling and wavering,
> undecided.
> Freed—the broken
> thermometer's mercury
> running away;
> and the rainbow-bird
> from the narrow bevel
> of the empty mirror,
> flying wherever
> it feels like, gay![47]

If this poem is reminiscent of Dickinson—the short line, breath-
less phrasing, hyphens, hummingbird imagery (see "A route of
evanescence"), nautical imagery (see "Wild Nights"—"Done with
the compass")—it also recalls—especially with its allusion to a
"wobbling and wavering" compass needle—the earlier poem
Bishop gave away in Ouro Prêto, with its centralizing notion of
norte and *nortear*. At the last the poet is free, free from her fret-
ful narcissism, it seems, free to feel free and free to be gay.

A fitting conclusion to any account of Elizabeth Bishop and
Brazil is the rehearsal of James Merrill's anecdote. He tells it
as having happened in 1970 in Ouro Prêto. "I was her first com-
patriot to visit in several months," Merrill recalls.

She found it uncanny to be speaking English again. Her other
guest, a young Brazilian painter, in town for the summer arts
festival and worn out by long teaching hours, merely slept in
the house. Late one evening, over old-fashioneds by the stove,
a too recent sorrow had come to the surface; Elizabeth,
uninsistent and articulate, was in tears. The young painter, returning, called out, entered—and stopped short on the thresh-
old. His hostess almost blithely made him at home. Switching
to Portuguese, "Don't be upset, José Alberto," I understood her
to say, "I'm only crying in English."[48]

The detail that Merrill left out of this retelling of his emblematic anecdote was that Bishop was crying over the loss of Lota
and the Brazilian life they had shared.[49]

9

The Adamastor Story

Elizabeth Bishop drew on Canto IX of *Os Lusíadas* for the notion of the "Island of Love" that she imagined was the land of "Santa Cruz" (Canto X, 140) the first Portuguese—"Christians, hard as nails, / tiny as nails, and glinting, / in creaking armor"— were culturally (though anachronistically) prepared to find when they landed in the place they called Rio de Janeiro, thinking they had come upon the mouth of a river.[1]

If Bishop found it natural for Portuguese sailors to expect to find a Camonean paradise in Rio de Janeiro, it is significant that Camões did not endow Vasco da Gama's sailors with any such paradisal expectations for Africa. From the beginning the Portuguese sailors find the African coast and so much of the interior as any of them get to see fraught with danger and foreboding. For all things and matters African are dominated, in Camões's poem, by the dangerous "Spirit of the Cape." The terrible Adamastor rules over the imagination of Gama and his men. The Cape of Torments must be doubled despite Adamastor and the real dangers and threats that emanate from him. And it is Canto V, with its vision of Adamastor—not Canto IX, with its celebration of the "Island of Love"—that has maintained a certain presence in the imagination of many Southern African writers. "The myth of Adamastor, which expresses the white man's anxieties about Africa," writes Stephen Gray, "occurs in a pattern that has continuity and development from the origins to the foreground of the literature."[2] The inner logic of that emerging pattern in the twentieth century can be discerned in the work of representative poets, from Roy Campbell's "Rounding the Cape" (1930) and Douglas Livingstone's "Adamastor Resuscitated" (1964) to David Wright's "A Voyage to Africa" (1976) and Charles Eglington's "The Blighter (after Fernando

Pessoa)" (1977), and in the fiction of André Brink. The sym-
bolic figure of Adamastor has come to stand for many things.
It begins as the symbol of African threat and danger to the European sailor, transforms itself into the symbol of the European
menace to Africa itself, and finally into the symbol of Africa
itself exploited by outsiders.

Preceding those twentieth-century Southern Africans who
employ Camões's Adamastor, however, are two nineteenth-century poets worth mentioning. The Scottish poet Thomas Pringle
(1789-1834), some of whose poetry was good enough to war-
rant Coleridge's praise, spent only a short time in Africa. To
Southern African literature he contributed one rather straight-
forward sonnet addressed to "The Cape of Storms":

> O Cape of Storms! although thy front be dark,
> And bleak thy naked cliffs and cheerless vales,
> And perilous thy fierce and faithless gales
> To staunchest mariner and stoutest bark;
> And though along thy coasts with grief I mark
> The servile and the slave, and him who wails
> An exile's lot—and blush to hear thy tales
> Of sin and sorrow and oppression stark:—
> Yet, spite of physical and moral ill,
> And after all I've seen and suffered here,
> There are strong links that bind me to thee still,
> And render even thy rocks and deserts dear;
> Here dwell kind hearts which time nor place can chill—
> Love Kindred and congenial Friends sincere.[3]

Already in this early poem, which ignores the mythicizing of
the Cape and concludes by celebrating the loving kindred and
congenial friends in Southern Africa, there is the clear recognition of the existence in Africa of "the servile and the slave"—
the "physical and moral ill" seen and suffered. This is the
naturalistic "cape of storms" with no mention of Adamastor.

John Wheatley, an economist who published his poems while
wintering at the Cape of Good Hope, died at sea in 1930 while
returning to England from India. His tribute to "The Cape of
Storms" was written during that last voyage. A rather bombas-
tic poem, running to two hundred sixty-four lines (in thirty-

three eight-line stanzas), it opens with an evocation of Camões's
monster of the cape:

> Spirit of Gama! round the stormy Cape,
> Bestriding the rude whirlwind as thy steed;
> The thunder cloud, thy car,—thy spectre shape
> Gigantic; who upon the gale dost feed
> And drink the water spout;—thy shroud, the skies;—
> Thy sport, the South and vast Atlantic sea;—
> Thine eye, the light'ning's flash!—Awake! arise
> From out the deep, in dread and awful sov'reignty!
>
> Now hast thou risen! By heaven it is a sight
> Most God-like, grand, and glorious to behold;
> Three elements contend, and fierce in fight
> As those who warr'd with mighty Jove of old.
> Oh, God! if any doubt thy being, or rate
> With vain and impious mind, at nought thy pow'r,
> So may it be such daring sceptic's fate
> To pass the Cape of Storms, when angry tempests lower.
>
> Do'st note the gath'ring clouds, as on thro' heav'n
> They speed their midway flight 'twixt sea and skies?
> Like to the first-born by the Archangel driv'n
> On earth, with flaming sword from Paradise.
> Do'st mark the spirit stirring of the deep,
> As onward sweeps the stormy hurricane;
> Rous'd like a roaring lion from his sleep,
> That wildly stares around, and shakes his shaggy mane?[4]

After considerable meandering through Western myth and European history, the poem reveals itself as a paean to the Cape
of Storms as a fit place and a fit monument for the poet's death
at sea battling against ferocious storms.

Pringle and Wheatley are precursors of the twentieth-century poet Roy Campbell. Unlike them, he was born and raised
in Southern Africa. Like Wheatley, he was well aware of
Camões's epic poem, as well as the story of Portugal's centrality in the Age of the Discoveries. "It was a Portuguese sailor
who first put South Africa on the geographical map," he began
a radio broadcast called "A South African Poet in Portugal." "It

was a Portuguese who first put South Africa on the literary map."[5]

Campbell is now best remembered by students of Portuguese literature for his translations from the Portuguese, including *Nostalgia: A Book of Poems* by Joaquim Paço d'Arcos, the minor twentieth-century Portuguese writer, and poems by Gil Vicente, Camões, Bocage, Antero de Quental, José Régio, Carlos Queiróz, and Fernando Pessoa.[6] As late as 1954, he announced that he was "translating an anthology of Portuguese poetry from the Troubadours to the present day, to be published simultaneously by the Portuguese government, who commissioned the work, and by the Harvill and Pantheon presses, respectively in London and New York."[7] In the last decade of his life he also turned his hand successfully to Eça de Queirós's fiction, publishing translations of the novels *O Primo Basílio* (*Cousin Bazilio*) and *A Cidade e as Serras* (*The City and the Mountains*) in 1953 and 1955, respectively.

It was his discovery of Luis de Camões that first brought Campbell to Portuguese poetry. *Os Lusíadas* struck him at once as a personally significant poem when he read it in 1926 in William Julius Mickle's eighteenth-century translation.[8] He kept the book beside his bed, he confided to his friend Edith Sitwell, along with San Juan de la Cruz.[9] As early as 1930 he had taken from Camões the title of his fourth book of poems, *Adamastor*, glossing the term in a note as "the spirit of the Cape whose apparition and prophecy form one of the finest passages in 'The Lusiad' of Camoens."[10] Indeed, Adamastor is one of the high points of Camões's great originality. In an essay in 1957, Campbell expands on this idea:

> There is nothing in his [Camões's] models to equal the terrifying grandeur of the apparition of the Spirit of the Cape of Good Hope, as the Giant Adamastor, or the prophetic truth of his allocution to the Portuguese argonauts of Vasco da Gama as they round the Cape of Storms for the first time. There is nothing in his models to equal the tender pathos of Camões' reference to Ines de Castro in the *Lusiads*. Passages like those describing the fighting at Melinde, the storms, the rounding of the Cape and the South Sea islands certainly owe as much to

his experience as a soldier and a sailor as they do to his reading. As well could Melville have written *Moby Dick* without the experience as Camões the *Lusiads*.[11]

Written in 1926 and first published in 1930, "Rounding the Cape" pays tribute to Camões's creation:

> The low sun whitens on the flying squalls,
> Against the cliffs the long grey surge is rolled
> Where Adamastor from his marble halls
> Threatens the sons of Lusus as of old.
>
> Faint on the glare uptowers the dauntless form,
> Into whose shade abysmal as we draw,
> Down on our decks, from far above the storm,
> Grin the stark ridges of his broken jaw.
>
> Across his back, unheeded, we have broken
> Whole forests: heedless of the blood we've spilled,
> In thunder still his prophecies are spoken,
> In silence, by the centuries, fulfilled.
>
> Farewell, terrific shade! though I go free
> Still of the powers of darkness art thou Lord:
> I watch the phantom sinking in the sea
> Of all that I have hated or adored.
>
> The prow glides smoothly on through seas quiescent:
> But where the last point sinks into the deep,
> The land lies dark beneath the rising crescent,
> And Night, the Negro, murmurs in his sleep.[12]

Campbell's biographer has written of the moment when the departing poet set down, in "Rounding the Cape," some of his "complex feelings towards his native land and her peoples. . . . Inspired by a last view of the stark coastal mountains of the Cape peninsula, the poem has all the bitterness and longing of the voluntary exile. For the first time Campbell can see South Africa whole. He personifies the country in Camoens's black giant Adamastor. . . ."[13] The poet is reminded not only of Africa's "spilled blood" and "broken . . . forests" but that "Night, the

Negro, murmurs in his sleep." In this poem Campbell offers
the strong characterization of Adamastor as symbol of a "dark"
and "dangerous" Africa that Southern African poets two generations later will see as the prevailing European symbol that
must be repudiated or at least reinterpreted from an African
point of view.

Campbell called Camões "the greatest of all South African
poets." "It is only Camões," he insists, "who gives one in words
a real sense of its awe [the sea's] and the grandeur of its stormy
seas [of 'going round Agulhas (or the Needles) to the Cape itself'] in that wonderful passage about Rounding the Cape."[14]

It is a sort of tribute to Campbell that Stephen Gray opens
his 1989 edition of the *Penguin Book of Southern African Verse*
with the Adamastor episode (Canto V) of Camões's *Os Lusíadas*,
in Richard Fanshawe's 1655 translation.[15] But the tribute is not
without irony, as Gray explains elsewhere. While *"The Lusiads*
is not the first and greatest South African poem," he writes, "it
is imperative to examine it by a reverse-angle shot, as it were;
we look at Camoens from the vantage point of the cruel, dark
and vengeful interior that he and his hero viewed as unfit for
human habitation."[16]

Little or no notice has been taken of Gray's rather extraordinary decision to claim Camões for South African poetry, and
to include in his anthology the canto of *Os Lusídas* which presents the terrifying Adamastor, tells of Portuguese encounters
with Africans, and narrates the story of Portuguese difficulties
in rounding the cape. It is as if, besides paying back an English
score, Gray is paying homage to Roy Campbell—a notion rein-
forced, perhaps, by Gray's further decision to follow the excerpt
from Fanshawe with Campbell's own translation of Camões's
verses "On a Shipmate, Pero Moniz, Dying at Sea." Gray's au-
dacious decision to include Camões in this late twentieth-century volume of Southern African poetry is put into perspective
and given considerable relief when one notices that not only is
Camões's poetry absent from the first version of the *Penguin
Book of South African Verse*, compiled by Jack Cope and Uys
Krige in 1968, but his very name goes unmentioned.

Why did Gray, who was born in Cape Town in 1941, decide

to include Camões's poetry as an example of Southern African verse? Gray explains that several of his selections are "historic in their own right."[17] As he sees it, Canto V of *Os Lusíadas* stands at the beginning of a sequence of literary history, one in which one poet's "epic of discovery gives way" to another poet's "domestic account of settlement."[18] Interestingly enough, Gray's "Southern African" literary history as reflected in this anthology also includes two other Portuguese poets: Fernando Pessoa (five poems) and Joaquim Paço d'Arcos (one poem).[19]

For an answer to the question of why Gray decided to set the lines and tone for his anthology by leading off with Camões, one must go elsewhere. There is no explicit answer anywhere in his anthology. But there is an answer available in his introduction to *Southern African Literature*, a critical history published in the United States in 1979. In Chapter II—"The White Man's Creation Myth of Africa"—Gray invokes John Purves's 1909 claim that Camões's "status in South African literary criticism" derives from his being "the father of white poetry in South Africa," only to take issue with Purves's further claim that *Os Lusíadas* "is not only the first but the greatest of South African poems. It is our portion in the Renaissance."[20] Against Purves, Gray argues:

> Less than one-tenth of it [*Os Lusíadas*] deals with experience in South Africa's territorial waters; Vasco da Gama, the hero of its epic voyage, was not trying merely to revisit Bartholomew Diaz's Cape of Storms. His objective was India and the Spice Islands, so that rounding the bottom of Africa was no more than a matter of clearing one more obstacle on a long course to glory. *The Lusiads* is the national epic of the Lusitanian bogeymen, the sons of its eponymous hero, Lusus, and not of any very significant number of South Africans.
>
> Nevertheless, with these qualifications clearly in mind, it is imperative to examine it by a reverse-angle shot, as it were; we look at Camoens from the vantage point of the cruel, dark and vengeful interior that he and his hero viewed as unfit for human habitation. Several of the characteristic themes of South African writing make rudimentary appearances in Canto V, and Camoens's dilemma was that of his white successors: how does a writer, at home in his own European literary environment, deal with essentially African experience?[21]

Although he had not intended it to function as such, Gray admits, Camões's most original creation, Adamastor, grew "to symbolize all the horrors and tribulations of Portuguese maritime history compressed into one."[22] He concludes:

> The figure of Adamastor is at the root of all the subsequent white semiology invented to cope with the African experience: he is menacing and inimical, and seen across a barrier; he belongs to an older but defeated culture, and is likely to sink the new European enlightenment if allowed within its purlieu; although his size is gigantic, his responses are essentially childish and they obey paternalistic directives; he is capable of love, but only carnally, so that if he advances too presumptuously he is to be humiliated and rendered impotent. . . . His Titanic force, tantamount to a block mountain's, his rumbling and earth-shaking, is not only the pent power of a vast and frighteningly unknown continent, populated by serpents and burning stones, but a symbol of the awe with which Africa was regarded in early experiences of the untamed.[23]

In short, "the myth of Adamastor . . . expresses the white man's anxieties about Africa."[24] To buttress this somewhat ahistorical generalization, Gray tracks the influence of Camões and the presence of his imagined Adamastor in the work of poets such as John Wheatley and Campbell, and in Douglas Livingstone's verse drama, *The Sea My Winding Sheet*, written in the 1950s. Gray also mentions other Southern African reworkings of the Adamastor myth, including Charles Eglington's "The Blighter (after Fernando Pessoa)." Although Gray does not discuss Eglington's poem in *Southern African Literature*, he does include it in the *Penguin Book of Southern African Verse*, where it is identified as "translated" from the Portuguese of Fernando Pessoa. Whether it should be considered a translation from Pessoa or an original poem "after" Pessoa's "O Mostrengo" from *Mensagem* (as it is so identified in Eglington's posthumously published *Collected Poems* in 1977)[25] does not matter so much at the moment as the text itself does, for it offers one more appearance of Adamastor in the poetry of Southern Africa:

> The blighter that is at the end of the sea
> On the pitch-black night raised itself flying;

Round the vessel it flew three times,
Three times it flew creaking,
And said, 'Who dared pierce
Into my dens that I do not reveal,
My black ceilings of the end of the world?'
And the helmsman said, trembling,
'His Majesty King John the Second!'

'Whose sails are these then which I rub against?
Whose the keels I see and hear?'
Said the blighter, and rolled three times,
Three times it rolled filthy and bulky,
'Who attempts what is solely my power,
I who abide where no one ever could see me
And who drip the fears of the depthless sea?'
And the helmsman trembled, and said,
'His Majesty King John the Second!'

Three times he raised his hands from the helm,
Three times he had them rooted on the helm,
And said after trembling three times,
'Here at the helm I am more than myself:
I am a People who wants the sea that is yours;
And more than the blighter, that my soul fears
And rolls on the darkness of the end of the world,
Orders the will, that ties me at the helm,
Of His Majesty King John the Second!'[26]

Historically, of course, it is the Adamastor myth's lasting influence on Southern African poetry—with its accrual of Euro-
colonialist baggage on both sides of the African question—that
justifies including Canto V of *Os Lusíadas* in this selection of
Southern African verse and turning Camões into a Southern
African poet, historically the first in a long line of such poets.
Politically, however, its justification is its potential usefulness
as Gray's stipulated symbol for Europe's "anxieties about Africa." In such a context and with such a design in mind, it hardly
matters that Camões's Adamastor has for centuries symbolized
the dangers of the ancient and well-named Cape of Torments—
"an apt symbol of the horrors which may well appal those who
break into waters where no men have sailed before"[27]—as it does

in the poems of John Wheatley, Roy Campbell, and Charles Eglington.

Adamastor serves a different purpose in David Wright's "A Voyage to Africa." "A myth, but the first immigrant European," Adamastor is invoked to bless the poem that will follow. Wright wants nothing less than a collaboration between himself and the "invented" giant spirit of the cape of storms who was turned into stone by a young woman. Like figures in a play, "gods or angels," Portuguese seamen, followed by the Dutch, made their "romantic" entries on the right side of the continent, and "thus began South African history." But on the "sinister" side sleep the bones of Dingann and his brother, threatening to awaken from their slumber to "discommode" the present plan in which "many blacks labour" to "make a white."[28] Wright's choice of the petrified Adamastor as his muse and guide and collaborator is not without its irony. But Adamastor as the first European myth of Africa remains intact.

But it is mock-heroically that Adamastor is handled in Douglas Livingstone's 1950s radio play *The Sea My Winding Sheet*. Taking his title from Wheatley's 1830 poem, Livingstone presents a mock-heroic Adamastor full of self-contradictions. "For Adamastor *'grande de membros'* like a colossus," writes Stephen Gray, "we now have Adamastor the perplexed buffoon."[29] In the section of *The Sea My Winding Sheet* entitled "Adamastor Resuscitated" is found the "giant of the Cape escarpment" personifying "the spirit of a disappointing European order rather than an African primitivism," as in Campbell's "Rounding the Cape."[30] Here is Adamastor whose collapse with his face forward in the sea forms the continent of Africa (in the words of Doris, Thetis' mother):

> Herakles counting corpses, near forgot,
> But searching, found and pulped the Giant's head
> As he lay dying, half-submerged by tides,
> This Giant, both with travail for his lot,
> Divided, doomed, was in confusion led.
> Around his shores my lovely Thetis rides.
> With thorn and grassy plain his form is draped.
> The continent of Africa is shaped.[31]

In *Cape of Storms: The First Life of Adamastor*—André Brink's
fable-like narrative of the early 1990s—however, Livingstone's
comic buffoon Adamastor is turned right-side-up into a sympathetic eponymous hero.[32] Again deriving from Camões's descriptive phrase for Adamastor—"tão grande era de membros"
(Canto V, 40)—but this time exploiting its sexual connotations,
Brink's Adamastor possesses a monstrous phallus, whose ever-
increasing size renders him dysfunctional as a lover and con-
sequently as a leader of his people, too. He is, in Brink's view,
the comic eponymous hero for an Africa invaded and betrayed
by foreigners arriving and leaving, as the Portuguese did first,
in birdlike ships. Adamastor becomes the scapegoat hero, em-
bodying the strengths and the weaknesses of indigenous popu-
lations. Well-meaning, gullible, and generous to a fault, he lives,
finally, and dies the first of his many deaths for the love of a
white woman taken from the first white invaders. With this
elaborated fable Brink invents for modern Africa a myth sub-
stantiated by the psychology and character of the tribal cyno-
sure. He tells it from the point of view of the white man's
monster, thus rescuing Adamastor from his Eurocentric meanings. It is his African virtues and culturally sanative functions
that come to the fore as he lives his fatal love and endures his
death by execution at the hands of the invaders who have come
back to recover the woman.[33] He is in some ways a Franken-
stein monster or, better still, an Elephant Man, elevated or transformed into the inspirational source of meaning for a colonized
England. Brink's closely crafted fable puts Adamastor forth as
the eponymous hero of a parodic *Iliad*, told sympathetically,
not from the European side, but from the side of the victim-
ized and willfully misunderstood African.

Cape of Storms is part of the major work—*The Lives of
Adamastor*—that the protagonist of Brink's earlier novel *States
of Emergency* (1988) is trying to write.[34]

> The writer of *States of Emergency* may not have been able to
> complete *The Lives of Adamastor*, but it is a work that André
> Brink has been writing all his life—the stories of those who
> inhabit the country that Camões portrayed as the disfigured
> Titan, imprisoned by the goddess Thetis for aspiring to her (for-

bidden) love and for rebelling against the new gods. Brink's continuing theme has been the black man of Africa loving the white woman of Europe, rebelling against the tyranny of colonial rule, and being doubly punished for his presumption. He has worked variations on this story from the eighteenth century to the present, but the myth remains essentially the same. The black struggle for independence and human dignity, for the right to love and freedom, continues, and no escalation of white repression seems likely to break its spirit.[35]

Indeed, Camões's Adamastor is identified as the "originary image" of the enduring politics of Brink's country and its people.[36]

Whether Brink's work will succeed in bringing about the transvaluation of the symbol of Adamastor for Southern Africans is not at all certain. After all, Adamastor as the symbol of the despised European is so thoroughly understood by Southern Africans that one student of "English-language inscriptions of skin colour" in Southern Africa can entitle his opening chapter on "the black migrant worker" simply "Adamastor's Mighty Shade" and offer no explanation in the text of what he understands "Adamastor" to signify.[37] Nevertheless, like so many earlier poems (but especially Elizabeth Bishop's "Brazil: January 1, 1502"), Brink's *Cape of Storms: The First Life of Adamastor* exemplifies that kind of revisionist history deriving from the play of the skeptical poet's imagination over facts and myths surrounding Camões's life and embodied in his work.

10

"Alma Minha Gentil" in English

It is not known when William Wordsworth composed "Scorn not the Sonnet,"[1] but by the time he published it, in 1827, Camões's lyric poetry had been available in English, and much appreciated, for at least two generations. Various translations of Camões's sonnets, odes, *redondilhas*, and songs had been published by William Hayley, Felicia Hemans, Lord Viscount Strangford, Robert Southey, and John Adamson. In *English Bards and Scotch Reviewers* (1809) Byron had already criticized Strangford's translations and possibly Southey's as well. Of Strangford he wrote: "Think'st thou to gain thy verse a higher place / By dressing Camoens in a suit of lace?" (lines 303-304) and "Let MOORE still sigh; let STRANGFORD steal from MOORE, / And swear that CAMOENS sang such notes of yore" (lines 921-922).[2] Of Southey, in the same poem, he wrote: "Behold the Ballad-monger SOUTHEY rise! / To him let CAMOENS, MILTON, TASSO yield" (lines 202-203).[3] In "Stanzas to a Lady, With the Poems of Camoens," Byron wrote:

> He was, in sooth, a genuine bard;
> His was no faint fictitious flame;
> Like his, may love be thy reward;
> But not thy hapless fate the same.[4]

In Southey and Felicia Hemans, Byron could have found translations of Camões's sonnet "Alma minha gentil." These were not the first English versions of Camões's most famous sonnet, however, for one such translation (of anonymous authority) was published in the eighteenth century by William Blake's sometime patron William Hayley.

In the original, the sonnet Sir Richard Burton describes as "the *chef d'oeuvre*" of Camões and Jorge de Sena calls "the most celebrated poem in the Portuguese tongue," reads:[5]

Alma minha gentil, que te partiste
    Tão cedo desta vida, descontente,
    Repousa lá no Céu eternamente
    E viva eu cá na terra sempre triste.
Se lá no assento etéreo, onde subiste,
    Memória desta vida se consente,
    Não te esqueças daquele amor ardente
    Que já nos olhos meus tão puro viste.
E se vires que pode merecer-te
    Algũa cousa a dor que me ficou
    Da mágoa, sem remédio, de perder-te,
Roga a Deus, que teus anos encurtou,
    Que tão cedo de cá me leve a ver-te,
    Quão cedo de meus olhos te levou.[6]

Whether one considers "Alma minha gentil" to be a more or less directly autobiographical response to an event crucial to Camões's sentimental life;[7] a craftsman's exercise in handling a topos, a neo-Platonic lyric on the separation of the soul from the body; or even a calculated re-writing of Petrarch (the poem's first two lines are literal translations of lines in Petrarch);[8] there is no gainsaying that this sonnet has evoked both far more popular and scholarly attention than any other Portuguese lyric of its or any other era. "On the most celebrated of Camões's sonnets, and without doubt one of the most beautiful sonnets in the world," Jorge de Sena has said, "much has been written, above all in critical ecstasy."[9] Such celebration, if not ecstasy, is reflected, albeit quietly, in the fact that over the last two centuries this poem has been translated into numerous languages.[10] English poets and writers alone have published at least (by current count) eighteen versions of the poem in English. The difficulty of translating it into English was pointed out by the anonymous reviewer in the London *Graphic* of J.J. Aubertin's *Seventy Sonnets of Camoens* in 1881:

[W]e take the famous and difficult No. XIX., and of it the first quatrain. [Robert] Southey renders it:—

Meek spirit who so early didst depart
  Thou art at rest in heaven! I linger here,
And feed the lonely anguish of my heart;
  Thinking of all that made existence dear, &c.

Mr. [William] Hayley's ("Anon"), like the Poet-Laureate, translates the whole into alternate elegiacs, in the so-called
Shakespearean sonnet, which is *magnifique*, but in nowise a sonnet:—

Go, gentle spirit! now supremely blest
  From sting of pain and struggling virtue go.
From thy immortal seat of heavenly rest
  Behold me lingering in a world of woe.

This is but a schoolboy's exercise in prosody without an atom
of the original *cachet*.
    Captain [Richard] Burton, in the *Athenaeum* (Feb. 26th),
has:—

Ah, gentle soul of me that didst depart
  This life of discontent, so sudden ta'en,
  Rest there eternal in the heavenly reign,
Live I here pent to play sad mortal part!

Mr. Aubertin writes:—

My gentle spirit! thou who hast departed
  So early, of this life in discontent,
  Rest thou there ever, in heaven's firmament,
While I live here on earth all broken-hearted, &c.

This is a great success: it renders not only the sense but even
the sound of the Portuguese.[11]

Of the English versions of "Alma minha gentil" that have
been located, one dates from the eighteenth century, seven from
the nineteenth, and ten from the twentieth. At least one is translated by a woman—Felicia Hemans. Two remain anonymous,
while one is the work of a South African. Richard Burton, the
English translator of *The Book of the Thousand Nights and a
Night*, translated Camões's sonnet twice. Among the better

known translators of the remaining twelve are Robert Southey (the Poet Laureate of England), Aubrey F.G. Bell (the Lusophile, scholar, and editor of the 1925 *Oxford Book of Portuguese Verse*), Keith Bosley, and Jonathan Griffin (the English poet known for translating Fernando Pessoa). Pessoa himself—educated in South Africa—translated Camões's sonnet.

That Pessoa even attempted a translation calls for brief comment. In an unpublished document composed, possibly, in 1912, Pessoa writes about the impossibility of translating poetry: "for a final and most flagrant example, we have Camões's celebrated sonnet, 'Alma minha gentil.' No translation can enable any foreigner to comprehend the basis of the beauty of that language without image, metaphor or 'phrasing,' that direct and simple language, when it is exactly therein that the beauty of the poem lies, at one with a lyrical movement continuous and intimate with its unbroken and dolorous rhythym."[12]

One of Pessoa's heteronyms, Álvaro de Campos, would have objected, perhaps, on other grounds. He publicly impugned the autobiographical sincerity of Camões's poem: "Camões laments the loss of his gentle soul; but finally the one who laments is Petrarch. Had Camões felt this emotion sincerely, he would have found a new form, new words—least of all the sonnet with its ten-syllable line. But no; he employed the decasyllabic sonnet even as during his life he might have worn black to show mourning."[13] Campos's statement might be taken as an answer to Aubrey Bell, who a decade earlier had written: "We may say that his [Camões's] *canções* are moulded on those of Petrarca, that in the sonnet *Aquella triste e leda madrugada* he is merely translating Virgil through Petrarca, and in the sonnet *Alma minha gentil* copying Petrarca and Guido Guidiccioni (1500-1541); but that does not explain Camões: no one who has read these poems will assert that they are imitative, they are too evidently sprung from a deep individual experience—*puras verdades ja por mim passadas*."[14] No one, that is, except Álvaro de Campos (though Pessoa had himself years earlier complained of the "pseudo-petrarchism of the sad poets of our Renaissance"[15]). Yet there is always the possibility that Campos's statement, stemming ultimately from Pessoa himself as the author of "Autopsicografia," is to be taken less as a criticism of Camões than as a perverse compliment of the kind Edgar Allan Poe used to pay competing writers. On the other hand, Álvaro de Campos may be calling for a "non-Aristotelian" aesthetic, one closer to that expressed by Ralph Waldo Emerson when he called for poetry that was a "meter-making argument," that is, expression that discovered its own form. Of course, despite Álvaro de Campos's complaint about Camões's Petrarchianism, he too, as Jorge de Sena reminds us, was wont to compose in sonnets.[16]

Presenting these eighteen translations of "Alma minha gentil" chronologically (by year of composition in one instance and by known first publication in all the others) seems both natural and useful in a particular way. Although it is unlikely that anyone taking up the task of translating this poem would have had at hand all or many of the antecedent translations, it is likely that in many (or at least some) instances, a given translator knew one or more of the versions with which a new version might compete. Moreover, whether the evidence at times indicates either appropriation or independently arrived at solutions, it is always interesting to see how certain words and phrases echo one or more of the extant translations. But the overall truth is that working from the same original text each translator offers a version that differs both from those that preceded it and those that follow it. Here is another illustration of how the same poem means different things to different people at different moments.

Most of these English versions of "Alma minha gentil" were done by poets of different stripe and magnitude. William Julius Mickle, Camões's second English translator, would have approved. "None but a Poet can translate a Poet," he explained, for "the freedom which this precept gives, will, therefore, in a poet's hands, not only infuse the energy, elegance, and fire of his author's poetry into his own version, but will give it also the spirit of an original."[17] Perhaps.

One textual variant calls for comment. In three of the early *Cancioneiros* that include poems by Camões, the second line of "Alma minha gentil" reads differently from the one quoted above ("tão cedo desta vida, descontente"), which appears in only one *Cancioneiro*. In those three *Cancioneiros*, the line reads, "tão cedo deste corpo descontente." On the basis of this—three ap-

pearances of "corpo" (body) and one of "vida" (life), Leodegário
A. de Azevedo Filho adopts the line in establishing the defini-
tive text of the poem.[18] This line offers support for a reading of
the poem in Baroque terms—"the harmonious binomial esthetic
of the Renaissance" between *alma e corpo*," that is to say, between soul or spirit and body.[19] Not one of the English translations given below reflects the alternative line adopted by
Leodegário Azevedo Filho. The body (read "the poet's body") is
never the site from which the spirit has departed.

1782

Go, gentle spirit! now supremely blest,
From scenes of pain and struggling virtue go:
From thy immortal seat of heavenly rest
Behold us lingering in a world of woe!
And if beyond the grave, to saints above,
Fond memory still the transient past pourtrays,
Blame not the ardor of my constant love,
Which in these longing eyes was wont to blaze.
But if from virtue's source my sorrows rise,
For the sad loss I never can repair,
Be thine to justify my endless sighs,
And to the Throne of Grace prefer thy prayer,
That Heaven, who made thy span of life so brief,
May shorten mine, and give my soul relief.

                                        Anonymous

[Anonymous. Included in William Hayley, *An Essay on Epic Poetry; in
Five Epistles* (London: J. Dodsley, 1782), 275. Reprinted in John
Adamson, *Memoirs of the Life and Writings of Luis de Camoens* (Lon-
don: Longman, Hurst, Rees, Orme, and Brown, 1820), 1:261. (See also
An Essay on Epic Poetry [1782] by William Hayley, facsimile repro-
duction with an introduction by Sister M. Celeste Williamson, SSJ
[Gainesville, Fla.: Scholars' Facsimiles & Reprints, 1968].)]

1803

Meek spirit, who so early didst depart,
Thou art at rest in heaven! I linger here
And feed the lonely anguish of my heart,
Thinking of all that made existence dear.
All lost! if in the happy world above,
Remembrance of this mortal life endure,
Thou wilt not there forget the perfect love
Which still thou seest in me, O spirit pure!
And if the irremediable grief,
The woe which never hopes on earth relief,
May merit aught of thee, prefer thy prayer
To God, who took thee early to his rest,
That it may please him soon amid the blest
To summon me, dear maid! to meet thee there.

Robert Southey

[Robert Southey, "Art. XXXII. *Poems, from the Portuguese of Luis de Camoens; with Remarks on his Writings, Notes, &c.* By Lord Viscount Strangford," *Annual Review* 2 (1804): 571. Reprinted in Adamson, *Memoirs of the Life and Writings of Luis de Camoens*, 1:94.]

1818

Spirit beloved! whose wing so soon hath flown
    The joyless precincts of this earthly sphere,
How is yon Heaven eternally thine own,
    Whilst I deplore thy loss, a captive here!
O, if allowed in thy divine abode
    Of aught on earth an image to retain,
Remember still the fervent love which glowed
    In my fond bosom, pure from every stain.
And if thou deemed that all my faithful grief,
Caused by thy loss, and hopeless of relief,
    Can merit thee, sweet native of the skies!
O, ask of Heaven, which called thee soon away,
That I may join thee in those realms of day,
    Swiftly as *thou* hast vanished from mine eyes.

                              Felicia Hemans

[Felicia Hemans, *Translations from Camoens, and Other Poets* (Oxford: J. Murray and J. Parker, 1818), 11. Reprinted in *Alma minha gentil, soneto de Camões com duas versões*, Camoniana No. 6 (Porto: Typographia Central de Avelino Antonio Mendes Cerdeira, 1884), seventh page, unnumbered. Included in *The Works of Mrs. Hemans*, with a memoir by her sister, and an essay on her genius, by Mrs. Sigourney, seven volumes (Philadelphia: Lea and Blanchard, 1842), 2:230, and in *The Poetical Works of Felicia Hemans*, memoir by Mrs. L.H. Sigourney (Boston: Phillips, Sampson, 1858), 96, as well as other editions of Mrs. Hemans's work.]

1845

Rest gentle soul, belov'd, who took'st thy leave
  So early from this world of sorrow;
  Rest ever blest in Heaven's bright morrow,
While comfortless in life's dark night I grieve,
But if remembrance of this life's allow'd thee
Where thou art gone in those bright realms above,
Ah ne'er forget the pure and ardent love
Which here below so constantly I show'd thee:
And if thou seest aught deserving thee,
  In this deep grief that in my bosom preys
Upon a heart yet aching to enfold thee,
  Implore the Almighty who cut short thy days,
To take me hence, as quickly to behold thee
  As from my weeping eyes, he did thee raise.

              Anonymous

[Anonymous. *The Lusitanian* No. 5 (1845) (Oporto). Reprinted in *Fragmentos dos Lusiadas e Sonetos Vertidos em Inglez* [Tiragem d'este primeiro numero do *Florilegio Camoneano*], (Porto: Livraria Camões de Fernandes Possas, 1877), fifty-third page, unnumbered.]

1873

My gentle spirit! thou who hast departed
So early, of this life in discontent,
Rest thou there ever, in Heaven's firmament,
While I live here on earth all broken-hearted;
In that Ethereal Seat, where thou didst rise,
If memory of this life so far consent,
Forget not thou my ardent love unspent,
Which thou didst read so perfect in mine eyes
And if, perchance, aught worthy thee appears
In my great cureless anguish for thy death,
Oh! pray to God who closed so soon thy years,
That He will also close my sorrowing breath,
And swiftly call me hence thy form to see,
As swiftly he deprived these eyes of thee.

                                        J.J. Aubertin

[J.J. Aubertin, *Seventy Sonnets of Camoens* (London: C. Kegan Paul, 1881), 17. Reprinted in *Sonnets from the Portuguese: A Volume of Translations*, selected and arranged by J. Silvado Bueno (Recife: Dutch-Alley Press, 1933), 9.]

1881

Ah, gentle soul of me, that didst depart
   This life of discontent, so sudden tane;
   Rest there eternal in the heavenly reign,
Live I here pent to play sad mortal part!
If from th' ethereal seats where homed thou art
   Thy mem'ry things of earth may not disdain,
   Forget not his dear love, whose ardent strain
Thou saw'st so pure in eyes that showed his heart.
And, if thou see my love claim aught of grace,
   If aught avail this everlasting care,
This yearning care no cure shall e'er displace;
   Pray Him who shorten'd those few years so fair,
As soon He bear me hence to see thy face
   As from mine eyes thy light so soon He bare.
Richard F. Burton

[Richard F. Burton, "Three Sonnets from Camoens," *The Athenaeum*, 2783 (26 Feb. 1881), 299.]

1884

My gentle Spirit! thou who didst depart
   This life of Miscontent so sudden tane;
   Rest there eternal in the heavenly Reign,
Live I pent here to play sad mortal part.
If in that happy Home, where throned thou art,
   Consent to memories of the Past they deign,
Forget not thou my love, whose ardent strain
Thou sawst in purest glance that spake my heart,
And if such love gain aught of grace fro' thee,
   If aught avail this woe wherewith I pine,
This pining woe that knows no remedy;
   Pray Him who shorted those few years of thine,
So soon He bear me hence thy sight to see
   As soon He bore thee fro' my sorrowing eyne.
Richard F. Burton

[Richard F. Burton, *Camoens. The Lyricks*, Part I (London: Bernard Quaritch, 1884), 37.]

1896

Soul of my soul, that didst so early wing
    From our poor world thou heldest in disdain,
    Bound be I ever to my mortal pain,
So thou hast peace before the Eternal King!
If to the realms where thou dost soar and sing
    Remembrance of aught earthly may attain,
    Forget not the deep love thou did'st so fain
Discover my fond eyes inhabiting.
And if my yearning heart unsatisfied,
    And pang on earth incurable have might
    To profit thee and me, pour multiplied
Thy meek entreaties to the Lord of Light,
    That swiftly he would raise thee to my side,
    As suddenly he rapt thee from my sight.

Richard Garnett

[Richard Garnett, *Dante, Petrarch, Camoens, CXXIV Sonnets* (Boston: Copeland & Day, 1896), 135.]

1913

Fair spirit in untimely banishment
Gone from me, quitting this sad life of woe,
Rest now in heaven may'st thou ever know
While upon earth in grief my life is spent!
If in the thoughts of those above is blent
A recollection of this life below,
May'st thou be mindful of that love's pure glow
That in my eyes for thee was evident!
And if the sense of my abiding grief
May merit any recompense from thee—
My sorrow for thy loss without relief—
Then pray to God that, as His swift decree
From my eyes bore thee after life so brief,
Even so now to thy sight it carry me!

Aubrey F.G. Bell

[Aubrey F.G. Bell, *Poems From the Portuguese* (Oxford: B.H. Blackwell, 1913), 39.]

1916

Soul of all gentleness, dear Soul, that spurning
this life so early and disdainfully,
now rests on high in Heaven eternally—
while I live here below, for ever mourning!—
If, in the seats of Heaven, whither thou'rt returning,
some memory of this life is given thee,
be not unmindful of that love bright burning
which in mine eyes thou yet may'st plainly see,
And, shouldst thou see there aught that can entreat thee
in this my pain, that ever with me stays,
then pray to God, who so cut short thy days,
that He, as quickly, take me hence to meet thee,
as He has taken thee now from my gaze.

George Young

[George Young, *Portugal, An Anthology*, preface by Theophilo Braga (Oxford: Clarendon Press, 1916), 85.]

1947

Oh gentle spirit mine that didst depart
So early of this life in discontent,
With heavenly bliss thy rest be ever blest
While I on earth play wakeful my sad part.
If in the ethereal seat where now thou art
A memory of this life thou do consent,
Forget not that great love self-eloquent
Whose purity mine eyes here showed thy heart.
And, if thou see aught worthy of thy light
In the great darkness that hath come on me
From thine irreparable loss' spite,
Pray God, that made thy year so short to be,
As soon to haste me to thy deathless sight
As from my mortal sight he hasted thee.

Fernando Pessoa

[Fernando Pessoa, in *Translation, Second Series*, ed. Neville Braybrooke and Elizabeth King (London: Phoenix Press, 1947), 34. Reprinted in Maria da Encarnação Monteiro, *Incidências Inglesas na Poesia de Fernando Pessoa* (Coimbra, 1956), 110; and *Numbers*, 3, no. 1 (Spring 1988): 7. According to José Blanco, it is also reprinted in L.S. Downes, "Object Lesson in Translation," *Cultura Magazine* (Sociedade Brasileira de Cultura Inglesa de São Paulo), no. 3 (May 1949), and in *A Manhā*, Supplement "Letras e Artes" [Rio de Janeiro], 3, no. 146 (4 Dec. 1949)— (*Fernando Pessoa: Esboço de uma Bibliografia* [Vila da Maia: Imprensa Nacional-Casa da Moeda/Centro de Estudos Pessoanos, 1983], 253).]

1947

My gentle heart, who didst so soon resign
This life in search of that more blest,
May'st thou for ever there in Heaven rest
And I in life-long sorrow here repine.

If there on that ethereal throne, now thine,
Remembrance be vouchsafed of this life's best,
Do not forget that love made manifest
To thee so purely from these eyes of mine.

And if ought worthy pity thou should'st see
In all the pain that ever with me stays
From the unhealing wound of losing thee,

Then pray to God, who so cut short thy days,
That hence to see thy face He may take me
As early as He took thee from my gaze.

Leonard S. Downes

[Leonard S. Downes, *Portuguese Poems and Translations* (Lisbon: Author's Edition, 1947), 32.]

1958

Dear gentle soul, who went so soon away
Departing from this life in discontent,
Repose in that far sky to which you went
While on this earth I linger in dismay.
In the ethereal seat where you must be,
If you consent to memories of our sphere,
Recall the love which, burning pure and clear,
So often in my eyes you used to see!
If then, in the incurable, long anguish
Of having lost you, as I pine and languish,
You see some merit—do this favour for me:
And to the God who cut your life short, pray
That he as early to your sight restore me
As from my own he swept you far away.

Roy Campbell

[Roy Campbell, *Portugal* (Chicago: Henry Regnery, 1958), 145. Included in *The Collected Poems of Roy Campbell*, vol. 3, *Translations*, foreword by Edith Sitwell (London: Bodley Head, 1960), 130-131; and Roy Campbell, *Collected Works*, vol. 2, *Poetry Translations*, ed. Peter Alexander, Michael Chapman, and Marcia Leveson (Craighall, S.A.: Ad. Donker, [Pty] Ltd., 1985), 317.]

1962

Gentle spirit mine,
Thou who didst depart this earth
Before thy time,
May'st thou be given rest eternal
With the bless'd,
Though I still bide in anguish
On this earth.
If, where thou dwellest
In the realm on high,
Memory be granted of this, our mortal life,
Forget not, I beg,
This heart that yearns within its breast for thee,
Nor the pure passion that flames so ardent
In these eyes.
If thou findest aught of worth
In this great love of mine that knows no cure,
Pray God, who cut thy mortal years so short,
At once to bear me hence to where thou art,
And, swift as thy sweet form was snatched from me,
May I once more behold thy features dear,
And feast upon them with these hungry eyes.

                           Henry H. Hart

[Henry H. Hart, *Luis de Camoëns and the Epic of the Lusiads* (Norman: University of Oklahoma Press, 1962), 150-51.]

1972

Gentle soul of mine, how swiftly thou has flown
away from life, so discontentedly,
taken thou thy rest there in heaven eternally,
may I live alway sad on earth alone.

If, having risen t'wards thy heavenly throne,
thou art allowed of life the memory,
do not forget that burning love for thee,
so pure, that in my eyes thou once hast known.

And if thou seest any cause that there can be
to merit thee in the grief that with me stays
of that heart-breaking loss without a remedy,

then pray to God, who thus cut short thy days,
to take me hence to see thee just as swiftly
as he carried thee aforetime from my gaze.

Arthur Reginald Barter

[A.R. Barter, *Portugal Through Her Literature: An Anthology of Prose and Verse* (Glastonbury: Walton Press, 1972), 139.]

1976

Gentle spirit, my own, who went and parted
So quickly from this life, unfulfilled so,
There in Heaven eternally repose
While I live here on earth always sad-hearted.

If memory of this life be permitted
There in the ethereal seat to which you rose,
Do not forget the burning love whose glow
So pure, in these eyes of mine, you once sighted.

And if some consolation ever seem to
You deserved by the grief flooding me through,
The hopeless heartbreak of you missing to me,

Implore God, Who has made your years so few,
As quickly to take me from here to see you
As He did quickly from my eyes take you.

                                        Jonathan Griffin

[*Camões[,] Some Poems Translated from the Portuguese by Jonathan Griffin[,] Essays on Camões by Jorge de Sena and Helder Macedo* (London: Menard Press, 1976). 'Gentle Spirit . . .' *verse and prose by Luis de Camões, Jorge de Sena, Eugénio Lisboa, Jonathan Griffin, Keith Bosley,* ed. Anthony Rudolf (London: Menard Press, 1980), 7.]

1990

To His Beloved In Heaven

O noble soul I love, who bade farewell
So fast to this life you were loth to leave
Rest there in heaven always, let me live
Here upon earth for ever sorrowful.

If there where you have risen, in the skies
A memory of this life is allowed
Do not forget that burning love which glowed
As pure as once you saw it in my eyes.

And should you see that some small merit there
May be obtained from all the woe that stays
From when your loss first choked me with despair

Ask God, O ask him who cut short your days
To lift me to your sight as fast from here
As then he lifted you beyond my gaze.

Keith Bosley

[*Luis de Camões: Epic & Lyric,* ed. L.C. Taylor, trans. Keith Bosley, illus. Lima de Freitas, with essays by Maurice Bowra, Helder Macedo, and Luis de Sousa Rebelo (Manchester: Carcanet/Calouste Gulbenkian Foundation, 1990), 75.]

1994

Oh gentle spirit too soon lost
to this body of discontent,
at eternal rest in the firmament,
and I, earthbound, forever lost
in sadness. If in that most
ethereal place, memories bent
on life here are allowed, shunt
not the pure burning love you must
have seen in my eyes, and if you
see merit in my fixed hurt at losing
you, petition Him, that God who
cut short your earthly being,
to return me as swiftly to you
as you were swept from my seeing.

George Monteiro

[George Monteiro, 1994, unpublished manuscript.]

Notes

Introduction

1. François-Marie Voltaire, "Idée de la Henriade," in *La Henriade*, in *Oeuvres Complètes de Voltaire*, nouvelle édition (Paris: Garnier Frères, 1877), 3; anonymous, "Camoens' 'Lusiads,'" *Graphic* 23 (5 March 1881): 227.

2. Erich Auerbach, *Introduction to Romance Languages and Literature* (New York: Capricorn Books, 1961), 185.

3. C.M. Bowra, *From Virgil to Milton* (London: Macmillan, 1945), 86.

4. Quoted in Richard Francis Burton, "Preface" to *Os Lusiadas (The Lusiads)*, "Englished" by Richard Francis Burton, ed. Isabel Burton (London: Bernard Quaritch, 1880), 1:xii. My translation of Corrêa's lines. Burton translates them: "Still by the Poets be the Poets read / Only be render'd by the Poet's tongue / Their works divine" (xii).

5. Ibid., xi.

6. *The New Encyclopædia Britannica* (Chicago: Helen Hemingway Benton, 1974), 3:703. Jorge de Sena's original Portuguese text appears in his *Trinta Anos de Camões* (Lisbon: edições 70, 1980), 1:295-304.

7. A.R. Milburn, *Penguin Companion to European Literature*, ed. Anthony Thorlby (New York: McGraw-Hill, 1969), 154.

8. See Maria Eugénia Igreja, "A Lírica de Camões em Língua Inglesa," in *Camões em Inglaterra*, coordinated by Maria Leonor Machado de Sousa (Lisbon: Ministério da Educação/Instituto de Cultura e Língua Portuguesa, 1992), 105.

9. Lord Viscount Strangford, *Poems, from the Portuguese of Luis de Camoens* (London: J. Carpenter, 1808), 36.

10. *New Letters of Robert Southey*, ed. Kenneth Curry (New York: Columbia Univ. Press, 1965), 1:352.

11. Henry H. Hart, *Luis de Camoëns and the Epic of the Lusiads* (Norman: Univ. of Oklahoma Press, 1962), 150.

1. Tasso's Legacy

1. *The Lusiad; or, The Discovery of India. An Epic Poem Translated from the Original Portuguese of Luis de Camoens* by William Julius Mickle (Oxford: Jackson and Lister, 1776), cli, note. Here and throughout the serif has been replaced with *s*.

2. Bowra, *From Virgil to Milton*, v.

3. Thomas R. Hart, "Luís Vaz de Camoëns (1524?-1580)," in *European Writers: The Middle Ages and the Renaissance*, ed. William T.H. Jackson and George Stade (New York: Scribners, 1983), 2:747-67.

4. Bowra, *From Virgil to Milton*, 139; Richard Fanshawe, *The Lusiads in*

Sir Richard Fanshawe's Translation, ed. Geoffrey Bullough (London: Centaur, 1963), 33.

5. Fanshawe, *Lusiads,* Bullough ed., 55.

6. Mickle, *Lusiad,* cxlviii.

7. Ibid., cxlvii-cxlviii.

8. Ibid., i.

9. Ibid., cliii. Emphasis added.

10. Ibid., viii. Emphasis added.

11. Curry, *New Letters of Robert Southey,* 1:337.

12. *The Poetical Works of William Wordsworth,* ed. E. de Selincourt and Helen Darbishire (Oxford: Clarendon Press, 1947), 4:372.

13. Ibid., 474.

14. See Markham L. Peacock, Jr., *The Critical Opinions of William Wordsworth* (Baltimore: Johns Hopkins Press, 1950), 363-64.

15. Mary Moorman, *William Wordsworth: A Biography: The Early Years, 1770-1803* (Oxford: Clarendon Press, 1957), 87, 99-100.

16. William Wordsworth, *An Evening Walk,* ed. James Averill (Ithaca: Cornell Univ. Press, 1984), 46.

17. *The Letters of William and Dorothy Wordsworth,* 2nd ed., 7, *The Later Years,* Pt. 4, *1840-1853,* rev. arranged and edited by Alan G. Hill from the first edition edited by Ernest de Selincourt (Oxford: Clarendon Press, 1988), 614.

18. *Shorter Poems, 1807-1820 by William Wordsworth,* ed. Carl H. Ketcham (Ithaca: Cornell Univ. Press, 1989), 67-68; and *The Prose Works of William Wordsworth,* ed. W.J.B. Owen and Jane Worthington Smyser (Oxford: Clarendon Press, 1974), 2:91.

19. *The Poetical Works of Wordsworth,* ed. Thomas Hutchinson, new ed., rev. by Ernest de Selincourt (London: Oxford Univ. Press, 1936), 206-7.

20. John Hollander, *Melodious Guile: A Fictive Pattern in Poetic Language* (New Haven: Yale Univ. Press, 1988), 92.

21. Ibid.

22. Burton, *Os Lusiadas,* 1:v. Isabel Burton's claim to authorship of this sonnet is made in her *The Life of Captain Sir Richard Burton* (London: Chapman and Hall, 1893), 2:181-82; Iolanda Freitas Ramos, "Camões Perfil Encomiástico em Inglês," in Machado de Sousa, *Camões em Inglaterra,* 232, n. 47.

23. Burton, *Os Lusiadas,* 1:ii; Mickle, *Lusiad,* cx.

24. Roy Campbell, "Luis de Camões," in *Talking Bronco* (London: Faber & Faber, 1946), 11.

25. Jonathan Griffin, "Camões Dying," in *"Gentle Spirit . . ." Verse and Prose by Luis de Camões, Jorge de Sena, Eugénio Lisboa, Jonathan Griffin, Keith Bosley,* ed. Anthonly Rudolf (London: Menard Press, 1980), 23.

26. Keith Bosley, *"Gentle Spirit,"* 24.

27. Born in Dublin, Richard Henry Wilde emigrated with his family to the United States in 1796, remaining, mainly in Georgia, for the rest of his life.

28. See George Monteiro, "'I Said "Frà Pandolf" by Design': A Note on Robert Browning's 'My Last Duchess,'" *Victorian Poetry* 23 (Summer 1985): 194-95.

29. These are reprinted in Edward L. Tucker, *Richard Henry Wilde:*

His Life and Selected Poems (Athens: Univ. of Georgia Press, 1966), 223-36.

30. Ibid., 278, n. 21.

31. Jeanne C. Howes mistakenly suggests that Melville, writing under a pseudonym, was the author of this translation. "Melville's Sensitive Years," *Melville & Hawthorne in the Berkshires: A Symposium,* Melville Annual 1966 (Kent, Ohio: Kent State Univ. Press, 1968), 37-38.

32. *The Poets and Poetry of Europe,* ed. Henry Wadsworth Longfellow (Philadelphia: Carey and Hart, 1845), 570-77.

33. Wilde's translations of four of Camões's sonnets are reproduced in Tucker's *Richard Henry Wilde,* 138, 139, and 151.

2. William Hayley's Patronage

1. S. Foster Damon, *A Blake Dictionary: The Ideas and Symbols of William Blake* (Providence: Brown Univ. Press, 1965), 176.

2. *Lord Byron: The Complete Poetical Works,* ed. Jerome J. McGann (Oxford: Oxford Univ. Press, 1980), 1:238.

3. David Bindman, *William Blake: His Art and Times* (London: Yale Center for British Art/The Art Gallery of Ontario, 1982), 144.

4. Thomas Wentworth Higginson, "The Literary Pendulum," in *Studies in History and Letters* (Cambridge: Riverside Press, 1900), 315.

5. Ibid., 315-16.

6. Damon, *Blake Dictionary,* 177.

7. *Memoirs of the Life and Writings of William Hayley, Esq.,* ed. John Johnson (London: Henry Colburn and Simpkin and Marshall, 1823), 2:139.

8. G.E. Bentley, Jr., *Blake Records* (Oxford: Clarendon Press, 1969), 72.

9. G.E. Bentley, Jr., *Blake Records Supplement* (Oxford: Clarendon Press, 1988), 15.

10. Bentley, *Blake Records,* 70; Morchard Bishop, *Blake's Hayley: The Life, Works, and Friendships of William Hayley* (London: Victor Gallancz, 1951), 265.

11. Bentley, *Blake Records,* 69. In an introduction to *The Heads of the Poets by William Blake (Eighteen in number—of which seventeen have not hitherto been published)* (Olney: Blake Society, 1925), Thomas Wright offers a list of twenty names: Homer, Euripides, Lucan, Dante, Chaucer, Ariosto, Spenser, Tasso, Ercilla, Shakespeare, Sir Philip Sidney, Camoens, Milton, Dryden, Otway, Pope, Blair, Cowper, Voltaire, and Thomas Hayley. Eighteen of them have survived. Those of Ariosto and Ercilla have disappeared.

12. *The Letters of William Blake,* ed. Geoffrey Keynes, (Oxford: Clarendon Press, 1980), 30.

13. Ibid., 30, n. 1.

14. K. Povey, "Blake's 'Heads of the Poets,'" *Notes and Queries* 151 (24 July 1926): 57.

15. Ibid.

16. Mickle is the authority for Johnson's statement. See *Boswell's Life of Johnson,* ed. George Birkbeck Hill, revised and enlarged edition by L.F. Powell (Oxford: Clarendon Press, 1934), 4:251.

17. *The Lusiad, or, Portugals Historicall Poem: Written In the Portingall Lan-*

guage by Luis de Camoens; and Now newly put into English by Richard Fanshaw Esq. (London: Humphrey Moseley, 1655).

18. *An Essay on Epic Poetry (1782) by William Hayley,* a facsimile reproduction, with an introduction by Sister M. Celeste Williamson, SSJ (Gainesville, Fla.: Scholars' Facsimiles & Reprints, 1968), 57-58.

19. Mickle, *Lusiad,* cx.

20. Hayley, *An Essay on Epic Poetry,* 273.

21. Strangford, *Poems, from the Portuguese,* 36.

22. Hayley, *An Essay on Epic Poetry,* 274-77.

23. Aubrey F.G. Bell, *Luis de Camões,* Hispanic Notes & Monographs: Portuguese Series (Oxford: Oxford Univ. Press/Humphrey Milford, 1923), 81.

24. John Adamson, *Memoirs of the Life and Writings of Luis de Camoens,* 2 vols. (London: Longman, Hurst, Rees, Orme, and Brown, 1820), 1:xi; see also 2:225-26.

25. Scholars still disagree on Camões's affliction. Was he blind in the left eye or the right? See, for example, Américo da Costa Ramalho, who asserts that Blake correctly portrayed Camões's blind eye as the right one ("Para a iconografia de Luís de Camões," in *Estudos Camonianos,* 2nd ed. [Lisbon: Instituto Nacional de Investigaçáo Científica, 1980], 89).

A concluding comment on the accompanying illustration of Blake's portrait of Camões (Fig. 1) is necessary. It is reproduced from *The Heads of the Poets by William Blake,* published in 1925 in a limited issue of twenty-five copies. Illustrations of the tipped-in portraits are individually tinted. Under the Camões plate, in a single line, appear three discrete phrases: (1) "One-eyed"; (2) "Accessory: An Anchor"; and (3) "'One of the best.'" It will be noted, however, that the Camões who appears here is not noticeably blind. On the contrary. Were it not known that he is blind in the right eye in the original painting, it would be the caption "One-eyed" that would seem most strange. It is possible that at some point between the first photograph of the original painting now preserved in the Art Gallery at Manchester (along with the other surviving seventeen paintings in the series) and the tinted plate in the Blake Society publication of 1925, Camões was refigured without his blind eye—left or right. The original photographs for *Heads of the Poets* were taken by Messrs. Flatters, Milbourne, and McKechnie of Manchester, but since each of the twenty-five copies of the tipped-in prints appears to have been individually tinted, it is possible that the artist painted in the "second" eye. That this might be a peculiarity of the one copy of *Heads of the Poets* at the Beinecke Library, Yale University, that I have been able to examine and from which the illustration used here has been taken can be ruled out, for the illustration identified as being reproduced from the "City of Manchester Art Gallery" and used in a 1990 publication on Camões shows what appears to be a two-eyed Camões (*Luis de Camões: Epic & Lyric,* ed. L.C. Taylor, trans. Keith Bosley, illus. Lima de Freitas, with essays by Maurice Bowra, Helder Macedo, and Luis de Sousa Rebelo [Manchester: Carcanet/Calouste Gulbenkian Foundation, 1990], 94). Curiously, the caption identifies Blake's "Camões" as an "engraving." It is odd that neither Thomas Wright nor anyone else responsible for the Blake Society's 1925 *Heads of the Poets* noticed the discrepancy between the photograph of the Camões painting and its caption describing Camões as "One-eyed," something that, later, Povey and L.C. Taylor also failed to detect. The Camões illustration used by Fanshawe in 1655 appears as Fig. 2.

26. John P. McWilliams, Jr., *The American Epic: Transforming a Genre, 1770-1860* (Cambridge: Cambridge Univ. Press, 1989), 55.

27. See Theodore Albert Zunder, *The Early Days of Joel Barlow: A Connecticut Wit* (New Haven: Yale Univ. Press, 1934), 218-19; Lewis Leary, "Joel Barlow and William Hayley: A Correspondence," *American Literature*, 21 (1949): 325-34; James Woodress, *A Yankee's Odyssey: The Life of Joel Barlow* (Philadelphia and New York: Lippincott, 1958), 245-66; and Arthur L. Ford, *Joel Barlow* (New York: Twayne, 1971), 46-84.

28. Joel Barlow, *The Columbiad: A Poem* (London: Richard Phillips, 1809), 8, note.

29. Ibid., 257.

30. Mickle, *Lusiad,* 205-6.

31. See Américo da Costa Ramalho, "Aspectos Clássicos do Adamastor," in *Estudos Camonianos,* 35-44. On the influence of Camões's Adamastor on Barlow's Atlas, see David Quint, *Epic and Empire: Politics and Generic Form from Virgil to Milton* (Princeton, N.J.: Princeton Univ. Press, 1993), 128-30.

32. Emory Elliott comments on the Atlas passage in *Revolutionary Writers: Literature and Authority in the New Republic 1725-1810* (New York and Oxford: Oxford Univ. Press, 1982), 118-21.

3. Elizabeth Barrett's Central Poem

1. Indicative of this neglect is Alethea Hayter's decision to include "Catarina to Camoëns" among the first poems mentioned in "Case for a Reassessment," the final chapter of *Mrs. Browning: A Poet's Work and Its Setting* (London: Faber and Faber, 1962), 227.

2. The poem has come down in at least five versions. It was first published in *Graham's Magazine* 24 (Oct. 1843): 208-9. Other versions can be found in Elizabeth Barrett Browning, *Hitherto Unpublished Poems and Stories* (Boston: Bibliophile Society, 1914), 2:185-86; *The Poets' Enchiridion* (Boston: Bibliophile Society, 1914), 47-49; *Diary by E.B.B.: The Unpublished Diary of Elizabeth Barrett Barrett, 1831-1832,* ed. Philip Kelley and Ronald Hudson (Athens: Ohio Univ. Press, 1969), 316-18; and *The Poems of Elizabeth Barrett Browning* (New York: C.S. Francis, 1854), 1:266-71.

3. *The Letters of Emily Dickinson,* ed. Thomas H. Johnson and Theodora Ward (Cambridge: Harvard Univ. Press, 1958), 2:575, and 3:759.

4. Strangford, *Poems, from the Portuguese,* 44. Melville's annotated copy, printed in 1824, is now in the possession of Professor J.C. Levenson of the University of Virginia. I quote, however, from the so-called "fifth edition," published in London in 1808. Melville's signed and annotated copy of the two-volume *Poems of Elizabeth Barrett Browning* (New York: Francis, 1860) is now in the Osborne Collection, New York Public Library.

5. *The Works of John Ruskin,* ed. E.T. Cook and Alexander Wedderburn (London: George Allen, 1909), 36:165.

6. Ibid., 197.

7. *The Letters of Elizabeth Barrett Browning*, ed. Frederic G. Kenyon (London: Smith, Elder, 1897), 2:200. Quoted in *Works of John Ruskin*, 36:197, note.

8. Quoted in Gardner B. Taplin, *The Life of Elizabeth Barrett Browning* (New Haven: Yale Univ. Press, 1957), 128, 234.

9. *The Letters of Robert Browning and Elizabeth Barrett Barrett, 1845-1846*, ed. Elvan Kintner (Cambridge: Harvard Univ. Press, 1969), 1:143.

10. Ibid., 241.

11. Ibid., 410.

12. *Poems of Barrett Browning*, 1:266.

13. *Letters of Robert Browning*, 1:563.

14. Ibid., 2:636

15. Ibid., 672.

16. Ibid., 959. When Robert objected that Elizabeth had over-praised his letters, she defended herself with an allusion to Camões: "And I offended you by praising your letters . . or rather *mine*, if you please . . as if I had not the right! . . . It is yourself who is the critic, I think, after all. But over all the brine, I hold my letters . . just as Camoens did his poem" (1:477). The allusion is to the legend that the shipwrecked Camões had saved the manuscript of his poem *Os Lusíadas* by holding it over his head above the ocean waves.

17. *Poems of Barrett Browning*, 1:267.

18. *Letters of Robert Browning*, 2:699.

19. *Letters of Robert Browning Collected by Thomas J. Wise*, ed. Thurman L. Hood (New Haven: Yale Univ. Press, 1933), 48; and *Robert Browning and Julia Wedgwood: A Broken Friendship as Revealed by Their Letters*, ed. Richard Curle (New York: Stokes, 1937), 99-100.

20. Taplin, *Life*, 234. Robert Browning's concern for Elizabeth's privacy was probably only half the story. Early on in his poetic career—stung by the public reaction to his "Pauline" (1833), a poem in which he Byron-like employed his own subjective voice—Browning had retreated into the poetry of dramatized, characterized, and named "voices" that were never to be confused with the poet's own voice. Hence his life-long predilection for the dramatic monologue and the dramatic idyll, poetry that enabled the poet to disappear behind his characterized speakers. In 1896 Edmund Gosse determined that "the name which was ultimately chosen, *Sonnets from the Portuguese*, was invented by Mr. Browning, as an ingenious device to veil the true authorship, and yet to suggest kinship with that beautiful lyric, called *Catarina to Camoens*, in which so similar a passion had been expressed." "Long before he ever heard of these poems," Gosse continues, "Mr. Browning called his wife his 'own little Portuguese,' and so, when she proposed, 'Sonnets translated from the Bosnian,' he, catching at the happy thought of 'translated,' replied, 'No, not Bosnian—that means nothing—but from the Portuguese! They are Catarina's sonnets!' And so, in half a joke, half a conceit, the famous title was invented" (*Critical Kit-Kats* [London: Heinemann, 1913], 3).

21. *Poems of Barrett Browning*, 1:270.

22. Quoted in Taplin, *Life*, 238.

23. Monica Letzring, "Strangford's *Poems from The Portuguese of Luis de Camoens*," *Comparative Literature* 23 (Fall 1971): 304.

24. Letzring, "Strangford's *Poems*," 289-90.

25. Ibid., 290. That others, besides Mickle, saw the shape of Camões's life quite differently and somewhat less romantically is attested to, for example, by Adamson's *Memoirs of the Life and Writings of Luis de Camoens*, a copy of which, incidentally, was presented to Robert Browning by his father on 9 October 1837 (see *The Browning Collections: A Reconstruction with Other Memorabilia*, compiled by Philip Kelley and Betty A. Coley [London/Winfield, Kans.: Armstrong Browning Library of Baylor University, 1984], 3). But Strangford's appealing view continues to have adherents; see Hart, *Luis de Camoëns and the Epic of the Lusiads*, 35-52 *et passim*.

26. Jorge de Sena, *A Literatura Inglêsa* (São Paulo: Cultrix, 1963), 182, note. The first English translation of *The Letters of a Portuguese Nun*, published in 1678, was the work of Sir Roger L'Estrange. His *Five Love-Letters from a Nun to a Cavalier* went into numerous editions. *Letters from a Portuguese Nun to an Officer in the French Army*, trans. W.R. Bowles, appeared in London in 1808, followed by editions in 1817 and 1828. The 1817, second edition of Bowles's translation was republished in New York by Brentano's in 1904. Among the many German translations of *Letters*, incidentally, is one by Rainer Maria Rilke in 1913. *Letters* even made it as a Haldeman-Julius little "Blue Book," in which series—the titles were then selling for ten cents each—William Gass read it, finding "Mariana Alcoforado, an overwrought and burdensome lady, certainly, whose existence I callously forgot until I read of her again in Rilke" (*On Being Blue: A Philosophical Inquiry* [Boston: David R. Godine, 1975], 4).

27. See F.C. Green, "Who Was the Author of the 'Lettres Portugaises'?" *Modern Language Review* 21 (April 1926): 159-67. Green's most trenchant piece of evidence for the French authorship of the *Letters* comes in his discovery of the original registration for printing, which reads: "Ce jourdhuy 17 novembre 1668 nous a été présenté à Paris le 28 octobre 1668 signé Mageret pour cinq années pour un livre intitulé *Les Valentines lettres portugaises Epigrames et Madrigaux de Guilleraques*" (162). As Green writes, "the important facts to note are then that the privilege was originally granted not for the *Lettres* alone, but for a *recueil* of the works of Guilleraques which included the letters; the author's name is given and there is no mention of translation; the name of the author is given as Guilleraques" (162).

28. *An Explanatory and Pronouncing Dictionary of the Noted Names of Fiction*, 17th ed., compiled by William A. Wheeler (Boston: Houghton Mifflin, 1882), 298. The first edition appeared in 1865.

29. Roger L'Estrange, *Five Love-Letters from a Nun to a Cavalier* (London: Printed for Henry Brome, 1678); quoted in Antonio Gonçalves Rodrigues, *Mariana Alcoforado: História e crítica de uma fraude literária*, 2nd ed. (Coimbra: N.p., 1943), 132.

30. Maude Bingham Hansche, *The Formative Period of English Familiar Letter-writers and Their Contribution to the English Essay* (Philadelphia: N.p., 1902), 54-55.

31. Margaret Anne Doody, *A Natural Passion: A Study of the Novels of Samuel Richardson* (Oxford: Clarendon Press, 1974), 23. Horace Walpole's French correspondent, Madame du Deffand, was not convinced of this. See *Horace Walpole's Correspondence with Madame du Deffand and Wiart*, vols. 1 and 2, ed. W.S. Lewis and Warren Hunting Smith; *The Yale Edition of Horace Walpole's Correspondence*, ed. W.S. Lewis, vols. 3 and 4 (New Haven: Yale Univ. Press, 1939), 3:54, 55, 87, 143; 4:152.

32. Doody, *A Natural Passion*, 18. William Henry Irving writes: "Letters have an important relation to the development of the novel and have told the story of fictitious adventure—especially amorous—from the time of the *Letters of the Portuguese Nun* or even the *Letters* of Abelard and Eloise down to the present. . . . Other collections of letters have fictional elements in them. Some forewarnings of Richardson's use of the letter form appear, containing slightly connected stories usually of the *Portuguese Nun* type" (*The Providence of Wit in the English Letter Writers* [Durham, N.C.: Duke Univ. Press, 1955], 13, 116).

33. E. Allen Ashwin, Introduction to *The Letters of a Portuguese Nun*, trans. E. Allen Ashwin (Talybont Dyffryn, North Wales: Francis Walterson, 1929), x. Jorge de Sena suggests the possibility that Browning's sonnets "from the Portuguese" offer a gloss on *Letters of a Portuguese Nun*. See *A Literatura Inglêsa*, 281-82, and Sena's annotative note (384) to A.C. Ward's *História da Literatura Inglesa*, trans. Rogério Fernandes, revised, annotated, prefaced, and completed for the "modern era" by Jorge de Sena (Lisbon: Estúdios Cor, 1959).

34. See Sena, *História da Literatura Inglesa*, 384 (note). It is also possible that Tennyson's poem "Mariana," despite its epigraph from *Measure for Measure*, owes a good deal to *Letters of a Portuguese Nun*. There, too, an anguished woman waits bootlessly for her lover or husband.

35. Strangford, *Poems, from the Portuguese*, 44.

36. Ibid., 10-13.

37. Ibid., 15.

38. Madonna Letzring, *The Influence of Camoens in English Literature*, *Revista Camoniana* 1-3 (1964-71), 3:122.

39. The author of several volumes of poetry, Felicia Dorothea Hemans (1793-1835) maintained a major reputation throughout much of the nineteenth century. But today she is not even remembered as the poet whose "Casabianca" tells the story of the boy who "stood on the burning deck."

40. Quoted in Letzring, "Strangford's *Poems*," 302-3.

41. My translation.

42. *Diary by E.B.B.*, 181, 188. The same experience informed a second poem, "Lady Geraldine's Courtship," another of Robert Browning's favorites among Elizabeth's poems, especially the lines (*Poems of Barrett Browning*, 2:152):

And this morning, as I sat alone within the inner chamber
With the great saloon beyond it, lost in pleasant thought serene—
For I had been reading Camoëns—that poem you remember,
Which his lady's eyes are praised in, as the sweetest ever seen.

Catalogue of Pictures, Drawings and Engravings . . . The Property of R. W. Barrett Browning, Esq. (Deceased) (London: Sotheby, Wilkinson and Hope, 1913) lists a copy of the 1804 edition of Strangford's *Poems, from the Portuguese,* "autograph signature of Robert Browning on fly leaf, calf." See also Kelley and Coley, *Browning Collections,* 49.

43. Quoted in William Irvine and Park Honan, *The Book, the Ring, & the Poet: A Biography of Robert Browning* (New York: McGraw-Hill, 1974), 153.

44. Irvine and Honan, *The Book,* 162.

45. Strangford, *Poems, from the Portuguese,* 27.

46. This description is that of Letzring, "Strangford's *Poems,*" 296.

47. This sentence, including the quotation from Strangford's *Poems, from the Portuguese,* comes from Letzring, "Strangford's *Poems,*" 297.

48. *Poems of Barrett Browning,* 1:268-69.

49. Fernando Pessoa, *Obra Poética,* 3rd ed., ed. Maria Aliete Galhoz (Rio de Janeiro: Aguilar, 1969), 639-43. My translation. Pessoa's translation appears to have been first published in Mario de Almeida's *Os Sonetos from the Portuguese e Elisabeth Barrett Browing* [sic] (Coimbra: Moura Marques, 1919).

4. Poe's Knowledge

1. Edgar Allan Poe, "Marginalia," *United States Magazine, and Democratic Review* 15 (Dec. 1844): 580-94; Edgar Allan Poe, *The Brevities: Pinakidia, Marginalia, Fifty Suggestions and Other Works,* ed. Burton R. Pollin (New York: Gordian, 1985), 178.

2. Poe, *The Brevities,* 179.

3. Edgar Allan Poe, *Southern Literary Messenger* 14 (Dec. 1848): 726; Poe, *The Brevities,* 452.

4. Theophilo Braga, *Bibliographia Camoniana* (Lisbon: Christovão A. Rodrigues, 1880), 63. My translation.

5. Ibid., 63-64.

6. *Curiosities of Literature* by I.C. D'Israeli, with *Curiosities of American Literature* by Rufus W. Griswold (New York: Leavitt, Trow, 1849), 23. The misspelling of Didot as Didet in this edition—an error that Poe does not commit—suggests that if D'Israeli is Poe's source (see Pollin's discussion of the matter in *The Brevities*), he drew his information from some edition other than the one I have employed.

7. Adamson, *Memoirs of the Life and Writings of Luis de Camoens,* 2:371-72.

8. Biographical and historical identifications for the various Leonors in Camões's work are suggested in João Franco Barreto, *Micrologia Camoniana* (Lisbon: Imprensa Nacional-Casa da Moeda/ Biblioteca Nacional, 1982), 459-60.

9. Adamson, *Memoirs of the Life and Writings of Luis de Camoens,* 1:291. My translation.

10. Fernando Pessoa, "O Corvo," *Athena* 1 (Oct. 1924): 27. My translation.

11. *Poems of Barrett Browning,* 2:181.

12. *Edgar Allan Poe: Essays and Reviews*, selected by G.R. Thompson (New York: Library of America, 1984), 128-29. Poe's emphasis.

13. *Collected Works of Edgar Allan Poe*, vol. 1, *Poems*, ed. Thomas Ollive Mabbott (Cambridge: Harvard Univ. Press, 1969), 356. Edward H. Davidson concurs; see his edition of the *Selected Writings of Edgar Allan Poe* (Boston: Houghton Mifflin, 1956), 506, note.

14. Mabbott, *Collected Works of Edgar Allan Poe*, 356.

15. *The Complete Works of Elizabeth Barrett Browning*, ed. Charlotte Porter and Helen A. Clarke (New York: Thomas Y. Crowell, 1900), 2:296.

16. Quoted in *The Poe Log: A Documentary Life of Edgar Allan Poe, 1809-1849*, compiled by Dwight Thomas and David K. Jackson (Boston: G.K. Hall, 1987), 591.

17. Davidson, *Selected Writings of Edgar Allan Poe*, 458; Strangford, *Poems, from the Portuguese*, 15.

18. Strangford, *Poems, from the Portuguese*, 15-16.

19. Davidson, *Selected Writings of Edgar Allan Poe*, 458.

20. Both Elizabeth Barrett and Edgar Allan Poe were contributors to *Graham's Magazine*. In fact, "Catarina to Camoëns" was published in *Graham's* in October 1843, "The Philosophy of Composition" in April 1846. Poe contributed regularly to *Graham's* beginning with its first number in January 1841 and until 1849.

21. Adamson, *Memoirs of the Life and Writings of Luis de Camoens*, 1:2-3. See also Aubrey Bell, who writes: "Probably the name was originally Camaño. Perhaps on the strength of a passage in Camões' lyrics . . . his name has been derived from the *ave que chamão camão* [that is, the bird they call *camão*]" (*Luis de Camões*, 108, n. 5).

22. *Diccionario Etymologico, Prosodico e Orthographico da Lingua Portugueza*, compiled by J.T. da Silva Bastos (Lisbon: Parceira Antonio Maria Pereira, 1912), 263.

23. *A Dictionary of the English and Portuguese Languages*, compiled by Anthony Vieyra (Lisbon: Rolland, 1861), 128.

24. Ibid. This is confirmed in *Diccionario Latim—Portuguez*, 14th ed. (Lisbon: Paulo de Azevedo, n.d.), 609.

25. Davidson, *Selected Writings of Edgar Allan Poe*, 103. Floyd Stovall glosses "Porphyrogene" as "Born to the purple." *Eight American Writers: An Anthology of American Literature*, ed. Norman Foerster and Robert P. Falk (New York: W.W. Norton, 1963), 64, n. 1.

26. Esther Rashkin, *Family Secrets and the Psychoanalysis of Narrative* (Princeton: Princeton Univ. Press, 1992), 129-30.

27. Elizabeth Barrett, who might have seen a source for Poe's poem in Robert Browning's "Porphyria's Lover," thought she recognized "madness" in Poe's speaker. "As to the 'Raven' tell me what you shall say about it!" she wrote to a friend on 12 May 1845. "There is certainly a power—but it does not appear to me the natural expression of a sane intellect in whatever mood; and I think that his should be specified in the title of the poem. There is a fantasticalness about the 'sir or madam,' and things of the sort, which is ludicrous, unless there is a specified insanity to justify the straws. Probably he—

the author—intended it to be read in the poem, and he ought to have intended it." (Quoted in *The Poe Log,* 531.)

28. Published in 1837 in installments in the *Southern Literary Messenger,* the magazine in which Poe's references to Camões and *Os Lusíadas* first appeared, *Arthur Gordon Pym* was brought out by Harper and Brothers of New York in 1838.

29. Edgar Allan Poe, "The Narrative of Arthur Gordon Pym of Nantucket," in Davidson, *Selected Writings of Edgar Allan Poe,* 405.

30. For a summary of the speculation regarding Poe's source for this figure, see *Collected Writings of Edgar Allan Poe,* vol. 1, *The Imaginary Voyages,* ed. Burton R. Pollin (Boston: Twayne, 1981), 356-59. Most recently, J. Lasley Dameron speculates that Poe's source was William Scoresby, Jr.'s *Journal of a Voyage to the Northern Whale-Fishery; Including Researches and Discoveries on the Eastern Coast of West Greenland* (1823). See *"Pym's* Polar Episode: Conclusion or Beginning?"* in *Poe's Pym: Critical Explorations,* ed. Richard Kopley (Durham and London: Duke Univ. Press, 1992), 33-43, 283-84.

31. Bowra, *From Virgil to Milton,* 126.

32. Luís de Camões, *Os Lusiadas,* ed. Frank Pierce (Oxford: Clarendon Press, 1973), 118.

33. Bowra, *From Virgil to Milton,* 123.

34. Fanshawe, *The Lusiad,* Bullough ed., 186.

35. Mickle, *Lusiad,* 205.

36. Voltaire, "An Essay on Epick Poetry," in Florence Donnell White, *Voltaire's Essay on Epic Poetry: A Study and an Edition* (1915) (New York: Phaeton, 1970), 108-9. Voltaire's English version was published in 1727, preceding its publication in French as *Essai sur la poésie épique* by a year. Kenneth Silverman sees Voltaire's *Zadig* as a possible model for the ratiocinative tale "The Murders in the Rue Morgue" (*Edgar A. Poe: Mournful and Never-Ending Remembrance* [New York: Harper Collins, 1991], 171).

37. Mickle, *Lusiad,* 206, note.

38. Bowra, *From Virgil to Milton,* 126. It should also be pointed out that available to Poe was Joel Barlow's description of Atlas in *The Columbiad.* (See chapter 2.)

5. Melville's Figural Artist

1. *White-Jacket or The World in a Man-of-War,* ed. Harrison Hayford, Hershel Parker, and G. Thomas Tanselle (Evanston and Chicago: Northwestern Univ. Press and the Newberry Library, 1970), 397.

2. Auberbach, *Introduction to Romance Languages,* 185.

3. See Lucy M. Freibert, "The Influence of Elizabeth Barrett Browning on the Poetry of Herman Melville," *Studies in Browning and His Circle* 9 (Fall 1981): 69-78.

4. Merritt Y. Hughes, "Camoens, 1524-1924," *New York Evening Post Literary Review* 5 (20 Sept. 1924): 1-2.

5. Lewis Mumford, *Herman Melville* (New York: Harcourt Brace, 1929), 58.

6. Newton Arvin, *Herman Melville* (New York: William Sloane Associates, 1950), 150.

7. Leon Howard, *Herman Melville: A Biography* (Berkeley and Los Angeles: Univ. of California Press, 1951), 73-74 *et passim*.

8. Jay Leyda, *The Melville Log: A Documentary Life of Herman Melville, 1819-1891* (New York: Harcourt, Brace, 1951), 1:172-73; 2:686.

9. Lawrance Thompson, *Melville's Quarrel with God* (Princeton: Princeton Univ. Press, 1952), 346-50.

10. *Moby-Dick or, The Whale*, ed. Luther S. Mansfield and Howard P. Vincent (New York: Hendricks House, 1952), 605 *et passim*.

11. Augusto Meyer, "Moby Dick," in *Prêto & Branco* (São Paulo: Instituto Nacional do Livro, 1956), 139-40.

12. Gilberto Freyre, *O Luso e o Trópico* (Lisbon: Comissão Executiva das Comemorações do V Centenário da Morte do Infante D. Henrique, 1961), 124-25; *The Portuguese and the Tropics*, trans. Helen M. D'O. Matthew and F. de Mello Moser (Lisbon: Executive Committee for the Commemoration of the Vth Centenary of the Death of Prince Henry the Navigator, 1961), 111-13.

13. Costa Ramalho, *Estudos Camonianos*, 114-20.

14. Brian F. Head, "Camões and Melville," *Revista Camoniana* 1 (1964): 36-77.

15. William H. Shurr, *The Mystery of Iniquity: Melville as Poet, 1857-1891* (Lexington: Univ. Press of Kentucky, 1972), 7, 229-32.

16. Edwin Haviland Miller, *Melville* (New York: George Braziller, 1975), 167-70.

17. George Monteiro, "Poetry and Madness: Melville's Rediscovery of Camões in 1867," *New England Quarterly* 51 (Dec. 1978): 561-65; and "Reason and/or Madness: Herman Melville's Rediscovery of Camões," *Revista Camoniana*, 2nd ser., 5 (1982-83): 39-48.

18. Freibert, "Influence of Elizabeth Barrett Browning on the Poetry of Herman Melville," 69-78.

19. Alexandrino Eusébio Severino, "The Adamastor and the Spirit-Spout: Echoes of Camoens in Herman Melville's *Moby Dick*," in *From Dante to García Márquez*, ed. Gene H. Bell-Villada, Antonio Giménez, and George Pistorius (Williamstown, Mass.: Williams College, 1987), 114-32.

20. McWilliams, *The American Epic*, 190-92, 215-16.

21. Mickle, *Lusiad*, i.

22. It was also the age of the advent of the steamship. In *Putnam's Monthly* 7 (June 1856): 644-58, one unidentified writer begins an article on "Our Light-House Establishment":

The protection of commerce is a serious thing; for modern science, skill, and enterprise have given to navigation a broad development, which makes past achievements shrink to insignificance. Over the three-fourths of the earth's surface, the pathless keel glides onward, and innumerable vessels weave a mesh of circling tracks around the world such as no Ariadne of the sea can unravel. To us, the Argonauts, Ulysses, Æneas, and all who, through the Pillars of Hercules, sought Atlantis, are only heroic by courtesy of the imagination. However we may admire Vasco, Columbus, or Cook, we cannot conceive any Camoens so insane as to frame a Lusiad in this age of steamers. [644]

23. Melville, *Moby-Dick*, 106.

24. What I have in mind is the possibility of developing further the connection touched upon by Severino as early as 1972 (see note 19) between the Old Man's speech at the end of Canto IV of *Os Lusíadas* and that of Elijah, the "ragged old sailor" Ishmael and Queequeg encounter as they leave the Pequod having just signed the ship's articles ("The Prophet," chapter 19 of *Moby-Dick*).

25. Howard P. Vincent, ed. *Collected Poems of Herman Melville* (Chicago: Hendricks House and Packard, 1947), 108.

26. Mickle, *Lusiad*, 211.

27. Hennig Cohen, ed., "Comment on the Poems," in *Selected Poems of Herman Melville* (Garden City, N.Y.: Doubleday, 1964), 195.

28. Robert Penn Warren, ed. *Selected Poems of Herman Melville: A Reader's Edition* (New York: Random House, 1970), 15, 74, n. 7.

29. Cohen, *Selected Poems*, 195; and Hennig Cohen, ed. *The Battle-Pieces of Herman Melville* (New York: Thomas Yoseloff, 1963), 206-7, 280.

30. Melville, *Moby-Dick*, 233.

31. Melville, *White-Jacket*, 96. Melville had read in Mickle's notes: "On the return of Gama to Portugal, a fleet of thirteen sail, under the command of Pedro Alvarez Cabral, was sent out on the second voyage to India, where the admiral with only six ships arrived. The rest were mostly destroyed by a terrible tempest at the Cape of Good Hope, which lasted twenty days. The daytime, says *Faria*, was so dark that the sailors could scarcely see each other, or hear what was said for the horrid noise of the winds. Among those who perished was the celebrated *Bartholomew Diaz*, who was the first modern discoverer of the Cape of Good Hope, which he named the Cape of Tempests" (Mickle, *Lusiad*, 208, note).

32. Vincent, *Collected Poems*, 202.

33. Head, "Camões and Melville," 65.

34. Mickle, *Lusiad*, 195.

35. Vincent, *Collected Poems*, 202.

36. Head, "Camões and Melville," 65.

37. Vincent, *Collected Poems*, 204.

38. See Richard F. Burton, *Camoens: His Life and His Lusiads*, 2 vols. (London: Bernard Quaritch, 1881), 2:651-52; and A. Bartlett Giamatti, *The Earthly Paradise and the Renaissance Epic* (Princeton: Princeton Univ. Press, 1966), 216, n. 19, *et passim*.

39. Vincent, *Collected Poems*, 228.

40. Adamson, *Memoirs of the Life and Writings of Luis de Camoens*, 1:148-49.

41. Henry Wadsworth Longfellow, *The Poets and Poetry of Europe*, new ed., revised and enlarged (Boston: James R. Osgood, 1871), 739.

42. Melville, *White-Jacket*, 270.

43. Cohen, *Selected Poems*, 232-33.
44. Howard C. Horsford, ed., *Journal of a Visit to Europe and the Levant* (Princeton: Princeton Univ. Press, 1955), 80, 102.
45. Cohen, *Selected Poems*, 233.
46. William Bysshe Stein, *The Poetry of Melville's Late Years* (Albany: State Univ. of New York Press, 1970), 110.
47. Cohen, *Selected Poems*, 233. Darrell Abel argues along similar lines in "'Laurel Twined with Thorn': The Theme of Melville's Timoleon," *Personalist* 41 (July 1960): 338. Shurr also attends to the familiar Melvillean theme of "diving": "'Grapple' here is not the same as 'wrestle' in the previous poem ["Art"], though one may be tempted to make a connection. The figure is different and, though innocent enough in appearance, one needs to pause at this word to consider the usual function of grappling hooks and dragging operations. The figure has much in common with Melville's consistent diving imagery and his feeling for the kind of reality one encounters in the depths" (*Mystery*, 243).
48. Mickle, *Lusiad*, cxii.
49. Ibid., 315. Voltaire repeats the story in his essay "On Epick Poetry" (1727): "in a Shipwrack on the Coasts of *Malabar*, he swam a Shore, holding up his Poem in one Hand, which otherwise had been perhaps lost for ever" (White, *Voltaire's Essay on Epic Poetry*, 108). Poets have been especially reluctant to give up the legend. A case in point is the Lisbon poet Cesário Verde (1855-1886), who writes in "O sentimento dum ocidental": "Luta Camões no Sul, salvando um livro a nado!" (*O Livro de Cesário Verde*, 2nd ed. [Lisbon: Europa-América, n.d.], 104).
50. Ralph, "Camoëns," *The Indicator* 1 (June 1848): 7. The author behind "Ralph" has not been identified, though "Ralph" was employed as "the name of a spirit formerly supposed to haunt printing-houses" (*An Explanatory and Pronouncing Dictionary of the Noted Names of Fiction*, 313).
51. Melville, *Moby-Dick*, 567.
52. Cohen, *Selected Poems*, 140.
53. Abel, "Laurel Twined," 335.
54. Cohen, *Selected Poems*, 232.
55. Ibid.
56. Strangford, *Poems, from the Portuguese*, 90. (Melville's copy is quoted by permission of J.C. Levenson.)
57. Shurr, *Mystery*, 270, n. 6.
58. *Poems*, vol. 16 of *The Works of Herman Melville*, Standard Edition (London: Constable, 1924), 414. Given the date and the general unavailability of the Constable edition, it will be useful to list subsequent reprintings of the poem: (1) *Collected Poems*, 380-81; (2) *The Portable Melville*, ed. Jay Leyda (New York: Viking, 1952), 740-41; (3) *Herman Melville*, ed. R.W.B. Lewis (New York: Dell, 1962), 373; (4) *Selected Poems of Herman Melville*, 168; (5) *Poems of Herman Melville*, ed. Douglas Robillard (New Haven, Conn.: College and Univ. Press, 1976), 245; and (6) Taylor, *Luis de Camões: Epic and Lyric*, 106. The poem appears in German in *Der Rosenzüchter und andere Gedichte*, ed. Walter Weber (Hamburg and Düsseldorf: Claassen Verlag, 1969), 39-40. The only Por-

tuguese translation is by Leonor Isabel Neves in "'Oiçam Camões': nos versos de Melville," *Jornal de Letras* (Lisbon) 11 (28 May 1991): 31.

59. Melville, *Moby-Dick*, 422.

60. Adamson, *Memoirs of the Life and Writings of Luis de Camoens*, 1:209-10. So widespread was the notion of an aging, infirm Camões that Byron could count on readers to understand perfectly what he writes about in "Stanzas to a Lady, With the Poems of Camoens":

> This votive pledge of fond esteem,
>   Perhaps, dear girl! for me thou'lt prize;
> It sings of love's enchanting dream,
>   A theme we never can despise.
> Who blames it, but the envious fool,
>   The old and disappointed maid?
> Or pupil of the prudish school,
>   In single sorrow, doom'd to fade?
> Then read, dear girl, with feeling read,
>   For thou wilt ne'er be one of those;
> To thee, in vain, I shall not plead,
>   In pity for the poet's woes.
> He was, in sooth, a genuine bard;
>   His was no faint fictitious flame;
> Like his, may love be thy reward;
>   But not thy hapless fate the same.

[McGann, *Byron: Complete Poetical Works*, 1:43-44.]

61. "Poems Unpublished by Melville," Houghton Library, Harvard University.

62. Baroness de Staël-Holstein, *Germany* (New York: Derby and Jackson, 1859); quoted in *The Melville Log*, 2:647. See Merton M. Sealts, Jr., *Melville's Reading*, revised and enlarged ed. (Columbia, S.C.: Univ. of South Carolina Press, 1988), 216.

63. Herman Melville, *Journal of a Visit*, 207, 225.

64. Strangford, *Poems, from the Portuguese*, 26.

65. Burton, *Camoens*, 1:32.

66. Mickle, *Lusiad*, cxlviii.

67. One wonders whether Melville was responding ironically to the fact that, unlike Camões, Tasso, and himself, even Mickle *the translator* had been, after his English patron's neglect, recognized and honored by the Portuguese, when he drew a vertical line in the right margin along the final sentence of this excerpt from Isaac Disraeli's *Curiosities of Literature* (1859), a book Melville acquired, signed, and dated "Feb 26 1862":

> Poor Mickle, to whom we are indebted for so beautiful a version of Camoens' Lusiad, having dedicated this work, the continued labour of five years, to the Duke of Buccleugh, had the mortification to find, by the discovery of a friend, that he had kept it in his possession three weeks before he could collect sufficient intellectual desire to cut open the pages! The neglect of this nobleman reduced the poet to a state of despondency. This patron was a political economist, the pupil of Adam

Smith! It is pleasing to add, in contrast with this frigid Scotch patron,
that when Mickle went to Lisbon, where his translation had long preceded his visit, he found the Prince of Portugal waiting on the quay to
be the first to receive the translator of his great national poem; and
during a residence of six months, Mickle was warmly regarded by every Portuguese nobleman.
[*Curiosities of Literature* . . . *A New Edition*, with an essay by B. Disraeli (London: Routledge, 1859), 83; quoted from Walker Cowen, *Melville's Marginalia*,
2 vols. (New York: Garland, 1987), 1:502.]

68. Norwood Andrews, Jr., *Melville's Camões* (Bonn: Bouvier Verlag, 1989).

69. Jorge de Sena, *Poesia de 26 Séculos* (Coimbra: Fora do Texto, 1993),
142.

70. Jorge de Sena, "Soneto de Torquato Tasso," *Ocidente* 35 (Nov. 1972):
38.

71. Jorge de Sena, *Trinta Anos de Camões*, 1:53. My translation.

72. Jorge de Sena, "Super Flumina Babylonis" (1966), in *Antigas e Novas
Andanças do Demónio* (Lisbon: edições 70, 1978), 179-92. The story appears
in English translation by Daphne Patai as the title story of *By the Rivers of
Babylon and Other Stories* by Jorge de Sena, ed. Daphne Patai (New Brunswick,
N.J.: Rutgers Univ. Press, 1989), 141-55. I am indebted to Antonio Feijó for
calling my attention to the exact way in which this story relates to my specu-
lations regarding Sena, Camões, and Melville.

73. See also Sena, *Trinta Anos de Camões*, 1:299. My translation.

74. It should be pointed out that in writing poems in the voice of Camões
both Melville and Sena were anticipated as early as 1655 by Sir Richard
Fanshawe, who included in his translation of *Os Lusíadas* his poem:

SPAINE *gave me noble Birth*: Coimbra, *Arts*;
LISBON, *a high-plac't loue, and* Courtly *parts*:
AFFRIC, *a Refuge when the* Court *did frowne*:
WARRE, *at an* Eye's *expence, a faire renowne*:
TRAVAYLE, *experience, with noe* short *sight*
Of India, *and the* World; *both which I write*:
INDIA *a life, which I gave there for Lost*,
On MECONS *waues (a wreck and Exile) tost*;
To boot, this POEM, *held up* in one hand
Whilst with the other *I swam safe to land*:
TASSO, *a sonet; and (what's greater yit)*
The honour to give Hints *to such a* witt:
PHILIP *a Cordiall, (the ill* Fortune *see!)*
To cure my Wants when those had new kill'd *mee*:
My Country (Nothing—yes) Immortall Prayse
(so did I, Her) Beasts cannot browze on Bayes.

[Fanshawe, *Lusiad*, Bullough ed., frontispiece.]

75. "Camões dirige-se aos seus contemporâneos" and "Camões Addresses
His Contemporaries" (trans. George Monteiro) in *In Crete with the Minotaur
and Other Poems* (Providence, R.I.: Gávea-Brown, 1980), 41-42.

76. See George Monteiro, "In Quest of Jorge de Sena," *Hispania* 70 (May 1987): 257-64.

77. [Isaac Disraeli], *Calamities of Authors; Including Some Inquiries Respecting their Moral and Literary Characters* (London: John Murray, 1812), 2:284-85.

78. Walter D. Kring and Jonathan S. Carey, "Two Discoveries Concerning Herman Melville," *Proceedings of the Massachusetts Historical Society* 87 (1975): 140.

79. Leyda, *The Melville Log*, 2:686.

80. Strangford, *Poems, from the Portuguese*, 90.

81. Ibid., 26.

82. Ibid., 27.

83. Head, "Camões and Melville," 68.

84. Strangford, *Poems, from the Portuguese*, 90. Strangford adds a suggestive note: "'*My senses Lost*,' etc. Perhaps this complaint was more than poetically true. The assertion in question might have been occasioned by the noble independence of our Poet's disposition, and by his undisguised contempt of titled ignorance and dignified barbarity. Such conduct will in all ages obtain the appellation of madness" (145).

85. Ibid., 27.

86. Vincent, *Collected Poems*, 380-81.

87. Strangford, *Poems, from the Portuguese*, 44.

88. Ibid., 58.

89. Ibid., 93.

90. See Miller, *Melville, passim*.

91. In this respect it is useful to recall that Edward Carpenter, the English poet-essayist and social activist best known in the United States for his defense of Walt Whitman's explicitly sexual poetry, included excerpts from *Typee* and *Omoo* in *Ioläus: An Anthology of Friendship*, a compilation of excerpts running from the Greeks to "modern times," first published in 1902. See also Robert K. Martin, *Hero, Captain, and Stranger* (Chapel Hill: Univ. of North Carolina Press, 1986), and Hershel Parker, "Historical Note," in *Moby-Dick or The Whale*, ed. Harrison Hayford, Hershel Parker, and G. Thomas Tanselle (Evanston and Chicago: Northwestern Univ. Press and the Newberry Library, 1988), 742.

92. Strangford, *Poems, from the Portuguese*, 96.

93. Ibid., 101.

6. Longfellow's Taste

1. This paragraph draws on my introduction to *The Poetical Works of Longfellow*, Cambridge Edition (1893; Boston: Houghton Mifflin, 1975), xvii-xxvii.

2. Edward Wagenknecht, *Henry Wadsworth Longfellow: His Poetry and Prose* (New York: Ungar, 1986), 226.

3. H.W. Longfellow, 31 May 1874, quoted in Harvey L. Johnson,

"Longfellow and Portuguese Language and Literature," *Comparative Literature* 17 (Summer 1963): 232.

4. Newton Arvin, *Longfellow: His Life and Work* (Boston: Little, Brown, 1963), 294. Wagenknecht calls *Poems of Places* "probably the most extensive anthology ever published in this country" (*Henry Wadsworth Longfellow*, 12).

5. *The Letters of Henry Wadsworth Longfellow*, 6 vols., ed. Andrew Hilen (Cambridge: Harvard Univ. Press, 1966-1982), 3:21.

6. This information on editions and reprints of *The Poets and Poetry of Europe* derives from Norwood Andrews, Jr., "Toward an Understanding of Camões' Presence as a Lyric Poet in the Nineteenth-Century American Press," *Luso-Brazilian Review* 17 (Winter 1980): 180-81; and "A Projecção de Camões e d'*Os Lusíadas* nos Estados Unidos da América," in *Estudos sobre a Projecção de Camões em Culturas e Literaturas Estrangeiras*, vol. 3 of *Os Lusíadas*, Edição Crítica, ed. Jacinto do Prado Coelho (Lisboa: Academia das Ciências de Lisboa, 1984), 331-449.

7. Arvin, *Longfellow*, 59. For a more recent assessment, set down in 1986, consider Wagenknecht: "One must admit that nobody in his America could have done *The Poets and Poetry of Europe* better than he did and that there were few who could have done it at all. As we examine the book now, we shudder for what it must have done to the eyesight of Longfellow's contemporaries, yet the fact remains that it was read and that it was one of the pioneering attempts to introduce Americans to European literature. W.P. Trent hardly exaggerated when he wrote that Longfellow 'was probably the most important link for almost two generations between the culture of the old world and that of the new.' As a people, we are still quite ignorant enough of Continental writers, but something at least has been accomplished, and we owe some of this to Longfellow" (*Henry Wadsworth Longfellow*, 225).

8. Longfellow, *Poets and Poetry of Europe* (1871), vi. He apologized for excluding "the Celtic and Sclavonic, as likewise the Turkish and Romaic," explaining that with those he was "not acquainted."

9. Hilen, *Letters of Longfellow*, 3:59.

10. Anonymous, "Early Literature of Modern Europe," *North American Review* 82 (Jan. 1834): 168. Interestingly, the author of this piece claims Camões and *Os Lusíadas* for Spanish literature, acknowledging that "this single work has secured to its author, like that of Cervantes, a permanent literary glory" (169).

11. J.C.L. Simonde de Sismondi, *Historical View of the Literature of the South of Europe*, 4 vols., trans. Thomas Roscoe (London: Henry Colburn, 1823), 4:250-51.

12. Longfellow, *Poets and Poetry of Europe* (1871), 731.

13. The other poets selected were Bernardim Ribeyro, Francisco de Portugal (Conde do Vimioso), Fernando de Almeyda, Gil Vicente, Francisco de Saa de Miranda, Antonio Ferreira, Pedro de Andrade Caminha, Diogo Bernardes, Fra Agostinho da Cruz, Fernão Alvares do Oriente, Francisco Rodriguez Lobo, Manoel de Faria e Souza, Violante do Ceo, Antonio Barbosa Bacellar, Francisco de Vasconcellos Coutinho, Pedro Antonio Correa Garção, Domingos dos Reis Quita, Claudio Manoel da Costa, João Xavier de Matos,

Paulino Cabral de Vasconcellos, J.A. da Cunha, Joaquim Fortunato de Valadares Gamboa, Antonio Diniz da Cruz, Francisco Manoel do Nascimento, Manoel Maria de Barbosa du Bocage, Antonio de Araujo de Azevedo Pinto Pereyra (Conde da Barca), Antonio Ribeiro dos Santos, Domingos Maximiano Torres, Belchior Manoel Curvo Semedo, Joam Baptista Gomez, José Agostinho de Macedo, João Evangelista de Moraes Sarmento, and J.B. Leitão de Almeida Garrett.

14. Longfellow, *Poets and Poetry of Europe* (1871), v. The single-volume Cambridge Edition of *The Poetical Works of Longfellow* contains only one translation from the Portuguese—"Song," from the Portuguese of Gil Vicente, which begins: "If thou art sleeping, maiden" (637).

15. I have followed Strangford's own identification of the works he translated, quoting the first lines as they appear in his book. For an illuminating study—makeup, reception, influence, and critical reputation—of Strangford's volume, see Letzring, "Strangford's *Poems*," 289-311.

16. In identifying the first lines of the works translated by Felicia Hemans I have used the Hernani Cidade edition of the *Obras Completas*, vol. 1, *Redondilhas e sonetos*, 4th ed. (Lisboa: Sá da Costa, 1971).

17. I have again used Hernani Cidade's texts when identifying the works taken from Roscoe's book.

18. Edgar Allan Poe, "The Philosophy of Composition," in Davidson, *Selected Writings of Edgar Allan Poe*, 455.

19. Mrs. Cockle's work first appeared in Adamson's *Memoirs of the Life and Writing of Luis de Camoens*. Adamson acknowledges "Mrs. Cockle, who obligingly versified his prose translations of those pieces which bear her initial" (xii). On this basis Madonna Letzring rightly attributes the work to Adamson with the "assistance of Cockle" (*Influence of Camoens*, 3:125). In *Poems of Places* Longfellow attributes them to Mrs. Cockle alone.

20. According to Letzring (*Influence of Camoens*, 3:124) William Herbert published the canzon "Vão as serenas águas" (as an ode) in his *Translations from the German, Danish, &c. to which is added Miscellaneous Poetry*, 2 vols. (London, 1806), 2:47-49.

21. Hilen, *Letters of Longfellow*, 1:389.

22. Ibid., 2:243.

23. Ibid., 6:15.

24. Ms letter, H.W. Longfellow to Jayme Batalha Reis, 3 May 1877, Biblioteca Nacional, Lisbon, Portugal. The complete letter appears in George Monteiro, "Two Longfellow Letters Not in Hilen's Edition," *Resources for American Literary Study* 17, no. 2 (1991): 263-64. The edition mentioned appears to be *Obras completas de Luiz de Camões*, edição crítica, 3 vols. in 2 (Porto: Imprensa portugueza, 1873-1874).

25. Jayme Batalha Reis, "Uma Visita a Henrique Wadsworth Longfellow," *O Occidente* (1 March 1880): 35-36. I am indebted to Dr. Pedro da Silveira for bringing this article on Longfellow, as well as Longfellow's letter to Batalha Reis, to my attention, and for graciously providing me with photocopies of both items.

26. Hilen, *Letters of Longfellow*, 6:302-3.

27. Ibid., 323.

28. Ibid.

29. Letzring, *Influence of Camoens,* 3:69.

30. Robert Southey, *Annual Review* 2 (1803): 575; quoted in Letzring, "Strangford's *Poems,*" 302.

31. Quoted in Johnson, "Longfellow and Portuguese Language and Literature," 231.

32. Curry, *New Letters of Robert Southey,* 1:352.

33. Arvin, *Longfellow,* 59.

34. Longfellow, *Poets and Poetry of Europe* (1871), 740.

35. Ezra Pound, *The Spirit of Romance: An Attempt to Define Somewhat the Charm of the Pre-Renaissance Literature of Latin Europe* (London: J.M. Dent, 1910). For a thoughtful critique of Pound's attack on Camões's work and his views on "the unmusical speech of Portugal" (*Spirit of Romance,* 228), see Norwood Andrews, Jr., *The Case Against Camões: A Seldom Considered Chapter from Ezra Pound's Campaign to Discredit Rhetorical Poetry* (New York: Peter Lang, 1988).

7. Higginson and Dickinson Tributes

1. Thomas Wentworth Higginson, "Emily Dickinson's Letters," *Atlantic Monthly* 68 (Oct. 1891): 453.

2. Johnson and Ward, *Letters of Emily Dickinson,* 2:519. Higginson writes to Dickinson in 1873, shortly after having visited her in Amherst.

3. Thomas Wentworth Higginson, "Portugal's Glory and Decay," *North American Review* 173 (Oct. 1856): 463-64.

4. Thomas Wentworth Higginson, "Letter to a Young Contributor," *Atlantic Monthly* 9 (April 1862): 410.

5. Unsigned [Valentine letter], *The Indicator: A Literary Periodical* 2 (Feb. 1850): 223-24. At the time *The Indicator* was edited by Dickinson's friend George H. Gould.

6. Quoted in Mary Elizabeth Kromer Bernhard, "Translating Emily Dickinson: In the Arts: Arts I," *Emily Dickinson International Society Bulletin* 4 (Nov./Dec. 1992): 8. "In its few brief years of existence," writes St. Armand, "[*The Indicator*] presented her [Dickinson] with a syllabus of courses in Romantic Gloom, Romantic Glory, and Romantic High Jinks, treating subjects as diverse as alchemy in Bulwer Lytton's *Zanoni,* the destiny of departed souls in 'Where are the Dead,' and the Transcendental toughness of Emerson's *Representative Men*" (Barton Levi St. Armand, "Emily Dickinson and *The Indicator:* A Transcendental Frolic," *Emily Dickinson Journal* 2, no.2 [1993]: 90-91).

7. Ralph, "Camoëns," *The Indicator,* 1:6.

8. *American Sonnets,* selected and ed. T.W. Higginson and E.H. Bigelow (Boston: Houghton Mifflin, 1890), vii-viii.

9. *Fifteen Sonnets of Petrarch,* selected and trans. Thomas Wentworth Higginson (Boston and New York: Houghton Mifflin, 1903).

10. Thomas Wentworth Higginson, *The Afternoon Landscape: Poems and*

Translations (New York and London: Longmans, Green, 1889), 105; reprinted in Higginson, *Outdoor Studies[,] Poems* (Cambridge: Riverside Press, 1900), 398.

11. Johnson and Ward, *Letters of Emily Dickinson,* 2:575.

12. Anna Mary Wells, *Dear Preceptor: The Life and Times of Thomas Wentworth Higginson* (Boston: Houghton Mifflin, 1963), 46.

13. Higginson, *Afternoon Landscape,* 106; reprinted in *Outdoor Studies,* 399.

14. Higginson, "Portugal's Glory and Decay," 474.

15. Thomas Wentworth Higginson, "The Origin of Civilization," in *Women and the Alphabet* (Cambridge: Riverside Press, 1900), 114.

16. Johnson and Ward, *Letters of Emily Dickinson,* 3:759.

17. Ibid.

18. It is possible that the allusion extends to the heroine of J.G. Holland's *Kathrina,* a poem that may also have provided a name for the Hollands' first grandchild.

19. Johnson and Ward, *Letters of Emily Dickinson,* 2:575.

20. *Poems of Barrett Browning,* 2:181.

21. Ibid., 2:152.

22. William H. Shurr, *The Marriage of Emily Dickinson: A Study of the Fascicles* (Lexington: Univ. Press of Kentucky, 1983), 125. See also Jack L. Capps, *Emily Dickinson's Reading, 1836-1886* (Cambridge: Harvard Univ. Press, 1966), 95, 167.

23. Josephine Lazarus, "Introduction" to *The Love Letters of a Portuguese Nun,* trans. R.H. (New York: Cassell, 1890), 22-23. As early as 1699, and for decades afterward, there appeared editions of the letters of Abelard and Eloise that included the letters of the Portuguese nun (see Rodrigues, *Mariana Alcoforado,* 108, 110ff).

24. Horst S. and Ingrid Daemmrich, *Themes and Motifs in Western Literature: A Handbook* (Tübingen, West Germany: A. Francke, 1987), 2. Other works in this tradition, all published after the first appearance of *Lettres portugaises* in 1669, are Charles-Louis de Montesquieu's *Lettres persanes* (1721), Claude Prosper Jolyot de Crébillon-fils, *Les égarements du coeur et de l'esprit* (1738), and the *Lettres de la marquise de M**** (1732).

25. Richard B. Sewall, *The Lyman Letters: New Light on Emily Dickinson and Her Family* (Amherst: Univ. of Massachusetts Press, 1965), 56. Elsewhere Sewall elaborates: "What is new about the letters is their sustained revelation of the intensity, depth, and power of her love and the agony of its frustration. As few have, she shows what it is to 'suffer' love" (*The Life of Emily Dickinson* [New York: Farrar, Straus and Giroux, 1974], 2:513). This is precisely what was said about *Letters of a Portuguese Nun,* beginning with the book's appearance in the seventeenth century. It seems to me that R.W. Franklin is too ready to announce: "Although there is no evidence the letters were ever posted (none of the surviving documents would have been in suitable condition), they indicate a long relationship, geographically apart, in which correspondence would have been the primary means of communication. Dickinson did not write let-

ters as a fictional genre, and these were surely part of a much larger corre-spondence yet unknown to us" ("Introduction" to *The Master Letters of Emily Dickinson,* ed. R.W. Franklin [Amherst, Mass.: Amherst College Press, 1986], 5). Franklin's "surely" is bravely offered but does not convince the reader who would want some direct evidence. And given the lack of evidence to support the claim, should not his assertion that Dickinson "did not write letters as a fictional genre" be stated with less assurance?

26. Green, "Who was the Author . . .," 162.

27. *Indicator* 2 (Feb. 1850); reprinted in Johnson and Ward, *Letters of Emily Dickinson,* 1:91-92.

8. Elizabeth Bishop's Black Gold

1. Elizabeth Bishop, "Love from Emily," *New Republic* 125 (27 Aug. 1951): 20-21; "Unseemly Deductions," *New Republic* 127 (18 Aug. 1952): 20.

2. Brett C. Millier, *Elizabeth Bishop: Life and the Memory of It* (Berkeley: Univ. of California Press, 1993), 237-41.

3. Bishop to Pauline Hanson, 12 Nov. 1951, Vassar College, Poughkeepsie, N.Y.

4. Vassar College.

5. Quoted in David Kalstone, *Becoming a Poet: Elizabeth Bishop with Marianne Moore and Robert Lowell,* ed. Robert Hemenway, with afterword by James Merrill (New York: Farrar, Straus and Giroux, 1989), 194.

6. Among Bishop's books now at the Houghton Library, Harvard University, is her underlined copy of Aubrey F.G. Bell's edition of the *Oxford Book of Portuguese Verse* (Oxford: Oxford Univ. Press, 1925). The Camões selection reflects only his work in lyric poetry.

7. Bowra, *From Virgil to Milton,* 128. Bowra continues: "When he [Camões] dreamed of an ideal garden, he was not altogether able or willing to deprive it of attractive inmates. So when Venus wishes to refresh the wanderers, she includes amorous pleasures among her benefits. Her Nymphs lure the sailors with song and dance, bathe in the streams or hide in the woods. The sailors catch glimpses of them and give pursuit. The Nymphs enter into the spirit of the sport, and, after suitable resistance, allow themselves to be captured" (128-29).

8. Mickle, *Lusiad,* 390-91. Emphasis added. Camões reads in the origi-nal:

> Pois a tapeçaria bela e fina
> Com que se cobre o rústico terreno,
> Faz ser a de Aqueménia menos dina,
> Mas de sombrio vale mais ameno. [9:60, ll. 1-4]

[Pierce, *Os Lusiadas,* 213.]

9. Fanshawe, *Lusiad,* Bullough ed., 291. Camões's original reads:

> Se lançam a correr pelas ribeiras.
> Fugindo as Ninfas vão por entre os ramos,
> Mas, mais industriosas que ligeiras,

Pouco e pouco sorrindo e gritos dando,
Se deixam ir dos galgos ancaçando. [9:70]
[Pierce, *Os Lusiadas*, 215.] Bishop's clipping of "Recessional," *New States-man* (17 Jan. 1964): 89—Christopher Hill's review of Geoffrey Bullough's edition of Fanshawe's 1655 translation of Camões's epic—is at the Houghton Library, Harvard University.

10. The sonnet was first attributed to Camões in the surviving index to the so-called *Cancioneiro do Padre Pedro Ribeiro* (1577), the manuscript of which was used by Barbosa Machado (*Biblioteca Lusitana*) but which was, it is said, destroyed in the 1755 Lisbon earthquake (see Hernani Cidade, preface to *Obras Completas*, xxxii-xxxiii). The sonnet appears fifteen years after Camões's death in the first edition of his lyrics, *Rhythmas*, published in 1595 in Lisbon by Manoel de Lyra for Estêuão Lopez, as well as *Rimas*, published in 1598 in Lisbon by Pedro Crasbeeck for Estêvuão Lopez. Leodegário A. de Azevedo Filho contests Camões's authorship but does not reject the sonnet outright; see *Lírica de Camões*, vol. 1, *História, metodologia, corpus* (Vila da Maia: Imprensa Nacional-Casa da Moeda, 1985), 285. Most students of Camões have found no reason to question his authorship; see, for example, Jorge de Sena, *Os Sonetos de Camões e o Soneto Quinhentista Peninsular,* 2nd ed. (Lisbon: edições 70, 1981), 88, n. 4.

11. Luís de Camões, *Lírica Completa*, vol. 2, *Sonetos,* preface and notes by Maria de Lurdes Saraiva (Vila da Maia: Imprensa Nacional-Casa da Moeda, 1980), 21. My translation.

12. Bishop, *Questions of Travel* (New York: Farrar, Straus and Giroux, 1965), vii.

13. For Bishop's translations of poems by Manuel Bandeira, Joaquim Cardozo, Carlos Drummond de Andrade, Vinícius de Moraes, and João Cabral de Melo Neto, see *An Anthology of Twentieth-Century Brazilian Poetry,* ed. Elizabeth Bishop and Emanuel Brasil (Middletown, Conn.: Wesleyan Univ. Press, 1972); for her translation of *Minha Vida de Menina,* see *The Diary of "Helena Morley"* (New York: Farrar, Straus and Cudahy, 1957).

14. Bishop to Loren and Lloyd Frankenberg, 17 Nov. 1965, Vassar College.

15. Frank J. Warnke, "The Voyages of Elizabeth Bishop," *New Republic* 154 (9 April 1966): 19.

16. Vassar College.

17. Lorrie Goldensohn, *Elizabeth Bishop: The Biography of a Poetry* (New York: Columbia Univ. Press, 1992): 193.

18. Quoted in Kalstone, *Becoming a Poet,* 150.

19. Bishop to Loren and Lloyd Frankenberg, 17 Nov. 1965, Vassar College.

20. Ibid.

21. Ibid.

22. *Poesias Escolhidas de Emily Dickinson,* trans. Olívia Krähenbühl (São Paulo: Saraiva, 1956).

23. Quoted in Kalstone, *Becoming a Poet,* 132.

24. Goldensohn, *Biography of a Poetry,* 69.

25. Millier, *Life and the Memory of It,* 384.

26. Lloyd Schwartz, "Annals of Poetry: Elizabeth Bishop and Brazil," *New Yorker* 67 (30 Sept. 1991): 85-97.

27. Untitled poem, in Schwartz, "Annals of Poetry," 86.

28. Quoted in Millier, *Life and the Memory of It,* 378.

29. Bishop, "Under the Window: Ouro Preto," in *The Complete Poems* (New York: Farrar, Straus and Giroux, 1969), 208-10.

30. Millier, *Life and the Memory of It,* 384.

31. Ibid., 368.

32. J.D. McClatchy writes of "One Art" (as well as some other poems): "It *shares* its subject with the person who reads and not just with the person written about" ("'One Art': Some Notes," in *Elizabeth Bishop* [Modern Critical Views], ed. Harold Bloom [New York: Chelsea House, 1985], 154).

33. In 1977 Bishop identified the lost houses in "One Art": "one in Key West, one in Petrópolis, just west of Rio Bay, and one in Ouro Prêto, also in Brazil" (interview with David W. McCullough, *Book-of-the-Month Club News* [May 1977]; reprinted in *Elizabeth Bishop and Her Art,* ed. Lloyd Schwartz and Sybil P. Estess [Ann Arbor: Univ. of Michigan Press, 1983], 309-10). Lota was of course intimately associated with the Brazilian houses.

34. Quoted in Millier, *Life and the Memory of It,* 523.

35. Millier asserts that "One Art" apparently grew out of the poet's "desperate fear of losing Alice [Methfessel]" but that "the poem is also Elizabeth's elegy for her whole life" (*Life and the Memory of It,* 506, 513).

36. Bishop, "One Art," in *Geography III* (New York: Farrar, Straus and Giroux, 1976), 31.

37. Goldensohn, *Biography of a Poetry,* 31.

38. See Millier, *Life and the Memory of It,* for an account of the evolution of "One Art" through an analysis of "the seventeen available drafts" of the poem (506-14); and Millier, "Elusive Mastery: The Drafts of Elizabeth Bishop's 'One Art,'" *New England Review* 13 (Winter 1990): 121-29.

39. Davidson, *Selected Writings of Edgar Allan Poe,* 38.

40. Roy Campbell, *Portugal* (Chicago: Henry Regnery, 1958), 143. The poem had appeared in *Talking Bronco,* where the opening lines read: "Camões, alone, of all the lyric race, / Born in the black aurora of disaster" (11). It is likely that Bishop was also influenced by Jay Macpherson's poetry in his *Welcoming Disaster* (Toronto: n.p., 1974), which includes poems entitled "Lost Books & Dead Letters" (10) and "Masters and Servants" (26). Bishop's copy of Macpherson's book is at the Houghton Library, Harvard University.

41. Goldensohn, *Biography of a Poetry,* 125.

42. Written on a copy of a page from the issue of the *New Yorker* printing "One Art," Vassar College. In Horácio Costa's translation of "One Art" into Brazilian Portuguese, "disaster" is readily rendered as "desastre" but "master" becomes "aprender"—to learn ("Uma Arte," in Elizabeth Bishop, *Poemas,* trans. Horácio Costa [São Paulo: Companhia das Letras, 1990], 207). Interestingly enough, when Jorge de Sena translated Campbell's sonnet on Camões, he employed the cognate words—"desastre" and "mestre"—in slant rhyme

("Luís de Camões," *Diario de Lisboa* [9 June 1952]: 3; reprinted in *Poesia do Século XX*, ed. and trans. Jorge de Sena [Porto: Inova, 1978], 402). The reader who brings a knowledge of Camões to "One Art" might well see in the "master-disaster" rhyme a sliding pun on Adamastor, the "Spirit of the Cape," whereas Dickinson's readers will recall that she addressed several "letters" of love and loss to an otherwise unidentified "Master."

43. *The Complete Prose of Marianne Moore*, ed. Patricia C. Willis (New York: Viking, 1986), 328.

44. Lloyd Schwartz, "One Art: The Poetry of Elizabeth Bishop, 1971-1976," in *Elizabeth Bishop and Her Art*, 150.

45. Goldensohn, *Biography of a Poetry*, 261.

46. Millier, *Life and the Memory of It*, 538.

47. Bishop, "Sonnet," in *The Complete Poems, 1927-1979* (New York: Farrar, Straus and Giroux, 1983), 192.

48. James Merrill, "Elizabeth Bishop (1911-1979)," in *Recitative: Prose by James Merrill*, ed. J.D. McClatchy (San Francisco: North Point Press, 1986), 122-23.

49. See *Remembering Elizabeth Bishop: An Oral Biography*, Gary Fountain and Peter Brazeau, comps. (Amherst: Univ. of Massachusetts Press, 1994), 266.

9. The Adamastor Story

1. Bishop, "Brazil, January 1, 1502," in *Questions of Travel*, 6.

2. Stephen Gray, *Southern African Literature: An Introduction* (New York: Barnes & Noble, 1979), 37.

3. Thomas Pringle, "The Cape of Storms," in *A New Book of South African Verse in English*, ed. Guy Butler and Chris Mann (Cape Town: Oxford Univ. Press, 1979), 17.

4. John Wheatley, "The Cape of Storms," in *The Penguin Book of Southern African Verse*, ed. Stephen Gray (England: Penguin Group, 1989), 58-59.

5. Roy Campbell, "A South African Poet in Portugal," in *Collected Works*, vol. 4, *Prose*, ed. Peter Alexander, Michael Chapman, and Marcia Leveson (Craighall, S.A.: Ad. Donker [Pty] Ltd., 1988), 434.

6. His translations of Camões include "The Sailor Girl" and "Canção VIII [*sic*]: Junto de un estéril, duro monte"—both in *Nine* 3 (Autumn 1951): 173-74. These poems are reprinted, along with an excerpt from *Os Lusíadas*, Book VIII, and the poems "On a shipmate, Pero Moniz, dying at Sea," "Seven long years was Jacob herding sheep," and "Dear gentle soul, who went soon away," in Campbell, *Portugal*, 137-45, and in *Collected Poems of Roy Campbell*, vol. 3, *Translations*, with a foreword by Edith Sitwell (London: Bodley Head, 1960), 124-31.

7. Campbell, "A South African Poet in Portugal," in *Collected Works*, 4:435. Campbell's editors note that "no such book appeared" (647).

8. Peter Alexander, *Roy Campbell: A Critical Biography* (Oxford: Oxford Univ. Press, 1982), 74.

9. Roy Campbell to Edith Sitwell, no date, Edith Sitwell Collection,

Harry Ransom Humanities Research Center, University of Texas at Austin.

10. Roy Campbell, *Adamastor* (London: Faber and Faber, 1930), 107.

11. Roy Campbell, "The Poetry of Luiz de Camões," *London Magazine* 4 (Aug. 1957): 30.

12. Campbell, "Rounding the Cape," in *Adamastor*, 38. Quoted with the permission of Ad. Donker (Pty), Ltd.

13. Alexander, *Critical Biography*, 74.

14. Roy Campbell, *Light on a Dark Horse: An Autobiography (1901-1935)* (London: Hollis and Carter, 1951), 174.

15. Gray, *Southern African Verse*, 1-26.

16. Gray, *Southern African Literature*, 17. See also David Quint, "Voices of Resistance: The Epic Curse and Camões's Adamastor," *Representations* 27 (Summer 1989): 111-41; reprinted in Quint, *Epic and Empire*, 99-125, 381-85.

17. Gray, *Southern African Verse*, xix.

18. Ibid., xxii.

19. The Pessoa poems are three from *Mensagem* (1934) ("O Mostrengo," translated as "The Blighter" by Charles Eglington; "Ascensão de Vasco da Gama," translated as "The Ascent of Vasco da Gama" by F.E.G. Quintanilha; and "Mar Portuguez," translated as "The Portuguese Sea" by Quintanilha); Alberto Caeiro's "Se depois de eu morrer," translated as "If, after I Die" by Jonathan Griffin; and the orthonymic "Azul, ou verde, ou roxo," translated as "Azure, or Green, or Purple" by Griffin. The Paço d'Arcos poem is entitled "Re-encounter" in Campbell's translation (208-9).

20. Gray, *Southern African Literature*, 15-16.

21. Ibid., 17.

22. Ibid., 24.

23. Ibid., 27-28.

24. Ibid., 37.

25. *Under the Horizon: Collected Poems of Charles Eglington*, ed. Jack Cope (Cape Town: Purnell, 1977), 9.

26. Gray, *Southern African Verse*, 167-68.

27. Bowra, *From Virgil to Milton*, 126.

28. David Wright, "A Voyage to Africa," in *A Book of South African Verse*, ed. Guy Butler (London: Oxford Univ. Press, 1959), 162-63.

29. Gray, *Southern African Literature*, 35.

30. Michael Chapman, *South African English Poetry: A Modern Perspective* (Craighall, S.A.: Ad. Donker, 1984), 74.

31. Douglas Livingston, "Adamastor Resuscitated," in *The Sea My Winding Sheet* (Durban: Univ. of Natal, 1971). Reprinted in *Theatre One: New South African Drama*, ed. Stephen Gray (Johannesburg: Ad. Donker [Pty], Ltd., 1978), 95-122. Quotation from Gray, *Southern African Literature*, 36.

32. André Brink, *Cape of Storms: The First Life of Adamastor* (New York: Simon and Schuster, 1993).

33. "What is at issue in a love story?" is posed and answered in Brink's earlier novel, *States of Emergency* (London: Faber and Faber, 1988): "In languages like Spanish and Portuguese the word for 'to love'—*querer* (besides *amar* of course)—is related to the concept 'to want' (cf. in English 'acquire',

'require'). Which would tally with our ordinary, superficial experience of love as a personal form of imperialism. But should one not, in addition, acknowledge in it some relation to words like 'quest' or 'request'? Love as ceaseless interrogation, as a search without end—not necessarily moving towards a Promised Land where sooner or later the pilgrim arrives, but a voyage which, in search of sense, demonstrates only the sense of search (i.e. the very fact that it is a *process*, an experience of being in motion, without any clearly defined point of departure or arrival)" (47). That this answer does not square with the political import of the rehistoricized story of Adamastor in *Cape of Storms* tells us how to approach the troubled narrator of *States of Emergency*.

34. Brink, *States of Emergency*, 2.

35. Andrew J. Hassall, "André Brink," in *International Literature in English: Essays on the Major Writers*, ed. Robert L. Ross (New York: Garland, 1991), 189.

36. Ibid., 182.

37. Michael Wade, *White on Black in South Africa: A Study of English-Language Inscriptions of Skin Colour* (New York: St. Martin's, 1993), 1-21.

10. "Alma Minha Gentil" in English

1. See chapter 1.

2. McGann, *Byron: Complete Poetical Works*, 1:238, 258. Byron seems to have in mind Thomas Moore's lines in "To Lord Viscount Strangford (Aboard the Phaeton Frigate, off the Azores, by Moonlight)," first published in *Poems Relating to America* (1806):

> Yes, Strangford, at this hour, perhaps,
>   Some lover (not too idly blest,
> Like those, who in their ladies' laps
>   May cradle every wish to rest,)
> Warbles, to touch his dear one's soul,
>   Those madrigals, of breath divine,
> Which Camoens' harp from rapture stole
>   And gave, all glowing warm, to thine.
> Oh! could the lover learn from thee,
>   And breathe them with thy graceful tone,
> Such sweet, beguiling minstrelsy
>   Would make the coldest nymph his own.

[*Poetical Works of Thomas Moore* (London: Longman, Brown, Green, and Longmans, 1852), 2:211.]

3. McGann, *Byron: Complete Poetical Works*, 1:235.

4. Ibid., 44.

5. Burton is quoted in Taylor, *Epic and Lyric*, 112; and Sena, in *Trinta Anos de Camões*, 2:136. My translation of Sena. Henry H. Hart echoes Sena: "They are the most famous verses in the Portuguese language, and are known to every Portuguese with the slightest pretense to education" (*Luis de Camoëns and the Epic of the Lusiads*, 150).

6. Camões, *Obras Completas*, 1:213-14.

7. See the note by Maria de Lurdes Saraiva (147) to *Luís de Camões, Lírica Completa*, vol. 2, and Hart, *Luis de Camoëns and the Epic of the Lusiads*, 150.

8. The lines in Petrarch are "Questa'anima gentil, che si diparte / Anzi tempo chiamata a l'altra vita." For discussions of Camões's debt to Petrarch in this sonnet, see Jorge de Sena, *Trinta Anos de Camões*, 2:109-12, and "O Heterónimo Fernando Pessoa e os Poemas Ingleses que Publicou," Sena's introduction to *Poemas Ingleses publicados por Fernando Pessoa* (Lisbon: Ática, 1974), 56-57. In both places—*Trinta Anos de Camões* (2:144, n. 40) and "O Heterónimo Fernando Pessoa" (57, note)—Sena calls attention to the primacy, in this regard, of Stanley Robinson de Cerqueira's article, "Adriano, Petrarca e Camões," in *Revista de Letras* (Assis, São Paulo), 2 (1961). In *Luis de Camões, Epic and Lyric*, however, Robinson's and Sena's arguments are implicitly rejected in favor of the sonnet beginning "Anima bella, da quel nodo sciolta."

9. Sena, *Trinta Anos de Camões*, 2:9. My translation.

10. According to Artur Forte de Faria de Almeida, "Alma minha gentil" had been translated, by 1972, into "mirandês, castelhano, galego, italiano, siciliano, bolonhês, veneziano, friulano, milanês, genovês, catalão, francês, inglês, alemão, vasconço, etc." (*Catálogo da Exposição Camoniana do Real Gabinete Português de Leitura do Rio de Janeiro Comemorativa do Quarto Centenário da Edição de OS LUSIADAS Seguido de notas Bio-Bibliográficas Sobre a Cultura Portuguesa do Século XVI* [Rio de Janeiro, 1972], 25).

11. Anonymous, "Seventy Sonnets of Camoens, &c.," *Graphic* 23 (2 April 1881): 323.

12. Fernando Pessoa, *Páginas de Estética e de Teoria e Crítica Literárias*, ed. Georg Rudolf Lind and Jacinto do Prado Coelho (Lisbon: Ática, 1966), 341. My translation.

13. Álvaro de Campos, "Nota ao Acaso," *Sudoeste* 3 (Nov. 1935): 7. My translation.

14. Bell, *Luis de Camões*, 101.

15. Fernando Pessoa, "Movimento Sensacionista," *Exílio* 1 (April 1916): 46. My translation.

16. Sena, *Trinta Anos de Camões*, 2:104.

17. Mickle, *Lusiad*, cl.

18. Leodegário A. de Azevedo Filho, *Lírica de Camões 2, Sonetos*, part 1 (Maia: Imprensa Nacional-Casa da Moeda, 1987), 95.

19. Ibid., 99, 112.

Index